PSYWAR

US pilots examine the fuse for an M16-A1 leaflet bomb in front of their black B-26 night intruder.

PSYWAR

Psychological Warfare in Korea, 1950–1953

Stephen E. Pease

STACKPOLE
BOOKS

Published by
STACKPOLE BOOKS
Cameron and Kelker Streets
P.O. Box 1831
Harrisburg, PA 17105

Printed in the United States of America

Cover design by Tracy Patterson

Cover photograph by Stephen E. Pease

Pen and ink drawings by Steven Rook

Photographs by Stephen E. Pease unless otherwise credited

First Edition

10 9 8 7 6 5 4 3 2 1

Library of Congress Cataloging-in-Publication Data

Pease, Stephen E.
    Psywar : psychological warfare in Korea. 1950–53 / Stephen E.
Pease. — 1st ed.
        p.   cm.
    Includes bibliographical references and index.
    ISBN 0-8117-2592-8
    1. Korean War, 1950–1953—Psychological aspects.   2. Psychological
warfare.   I. Title
DS921.5.P78P43   1992
951.904'2—dc20   92-21511
                                                                      CIP

To Peggy, Karie, and Kris
for their tolerance and understanding

Psychological warfare has been firmly recognized as an integral member of our family of weapons. While we realize fully that this mode of operation is not decisive by itself, it is also certain that, in combination with the conventional combat weapons, psychological warfare will contribute materially to the winning of wars.

Secretary of the Army Frank Pace, Jr.
Semiannual Report of the Secretary of the Army, 1950

CONTENTS

ACKNOWLEDGMENTS

I am indebted to the following Veterans of the Forgotten War for their help in providing information for this book. They unselfishly shared their experiences and memories as well as the quotes in chapters three through eight and all the leaflets pictured herein.

Chester Bair, 32nd Heavy Tank Co., 7th Inf. Div.; James G. Chapman, Co. B, 223 Inf. Reg., 40th Div.; George Crerand, 2nd Engineer, 2nd Inf. Div.; Jerome Clauser, Infantry, later researcher for 7th Psyop Group, 24th Psyop Detachment; Tom Drew, D-2-7, 1st Marine Div.; Roy Dunham, 21st TCS, 6th TCS; Thomas A. Evans, 999th AFA; Samuel Freeman, 1st RB&L, PWS; Paul R. Garland, 5th RCT; Harold W. Gilbert, 43rd TCS, 315 TCW, B Flight; Melvin N. Granos, 3rd Plt., Love Co., 35th CACTI Inf. Reg.; Edward J. Hanrahan, Jr., 3rd Inf. Div., 15th Inf. Reg., Co. B; Warren W. Harper Sr., Reg. Recon Plt., 187th ARCT; Richard Hughes, 21st TCS, Kyushu Gypsies; Bill Klopp, 6167th Ops. Sq., 6153rd Air Base Sq., 581st ARC; R. W. Koch, 581st ARC; Len Martin, Flame Plt., HQ Co., 1st Tank Bat., 1st Marine Div.; Marc Michalakes, 21st TCS, Kyushu Gypsies; Walter Morrison, Jr., 24th Div., MP Co.; David D. Phelps for his father; John Sonley, 5th Ind. RCT, M Co., 3rd Bat.; Marion Williams, 21st TCS, Kyushu Gypsies; Woody Woodruff, 1st Plt., Love Co., 35th CACTI Inf. Reg.

My thanks to the staffs of the National Archives (Still Picture) and the Air Force Museum and to the archival staff at the National Air and Space Museum.

INTRODUCTION

Psychological warfare is the attempt by one nation to gain an advantage over another by exploiting fear, mistrust, suspicion, rumor, prejudice, and what von Clausewitz identified as an often decisive principle of war, uncertainty, to influence international opinion and/or the frame of mind of opposing soldiers. The goal is to affect the enemy's mind and persuade him to take an action, even against his conscious will, that is favorable to his opponent.

Psychological warfare was a small part of the Korean War, but it remains a major part of the war's myth. Films in particular perpetuate the myth with scenes like these: Hordes of North Korean and Chinese soldiers run over the barren, shell-blasted hills at night, accompanied by bugles and shouts; huge loudspeakers plead with UN soldiers to throw down their weapons and go home; and the wily Oriental interrogation officer uses lies and deception as he talks to a downed US flyer, burning his wife's photo and letters to get him to talk. Or, a radio propaganda officer talks to US soldiers at an outpost on a freezing hill in a tone too heavy with persuasion, insincerity, and political diatribe about home and the girls they left behind, and wouldn't it be great to be there now? Just drop your arms and surrender, we will take good care of you, and you will see that girl again—familiar images from *Pork Chop Hill* and even *M*A*S*H*.

Korea is the forgotten war, just a police action between World War II and Vietnam. At the time, the American people were preoccupied with the threats of the Soviets overrunning Europe and the atomic bomb. We were unprepared for a real war in the Far East. We were very unprepared for an enemy that would take our sons and use them against us so easily.

PART ONE

PSYWAR in Military History

Psychological warfare in the Korean War was the result of the accumulated experience with psychological techniques from the earliest recorded conflicts in Greece and China to World War II. Specific PSYWAR units were established for Korea, and vigorous PSYWAR operations were pursued. Battles were planned with complementary PSYWAR operations, and for the first time, specific PSYWAR operations were planned that had no immediate battle counterpart. PSYWAR played an important role in the outcome of the war.

1

PSYWAR in Ancient and Modern Warfare

Psychological warfare uses mental bullets. It is bloodless and inexpensive, sometimes unethical, and often ineffective. It is an offensive weapon that attempts to exploit the enemy's weaknesses to further tactical or strategic ends. Like a real bullet, it doesn't care if it wounds. Unlike a real bullet, it can be used at home, too.

Psychological warfare has existed since records of war were first kept. Like prostitution, intelligence, and politics, it is one of the world's oldest professions. Ancient military commanders knew the value of psychological warfare. In Greece during the Persian Wars, according to Herodotus, the Persians had forcibly enlisted Ionian Greeks into their army. Themistocles, the Athenian commander, sent his men ashore to cut messages into the rocks for the Ionians urging them not to fight against the Athenians, just as both sides in the Korean War would urge their fellow Koreans. The messages were intended to inject uncertainty into the thinking of the Persian command. Would the Ionians honor their blood ties and refuse to fight against the Athenians? The doubt and suspicion that the messages caused weakened the Persian army because they were unable to trust the Ionians, and therefore did not use them to fight.

Various methods have been used to deliver PSYWAR messages. The medieval Chinese used kites to carry messages to their foes. During the European Middle Ages, archers tied to their arrows messages urging surrender and fired them into besieged castles. The French used silk and paper balloons to carry messages to opposing soldiers; the balloon released leaflets at intervals that were controlled by a slow fuse. Balloons have been used in more modern times by the Nationalist Chinese to send leaflets to the Communist mainland.

American PSYWAR is as old as the country itself. Leaflets were used during the Revolution to persuade British soldiers to desert, promising safe passage, good treatment, and other advantages. Leaflets were also distributed in Canada to persuade French-Canadians not to support the British, and leaflets in German were handed to Hessian soldiers, offering land in exchange for desertion. A German-speaking American carried the leaflets directly into the Hessian camp. The British also printed leaflets, exhorting Americans to stand by the legal authorities and to abandon the rebels. The leaflets were carried by infiltrators and patrols and were posted in British-held villages.

During the Civil War, newspapers and public proclamations were used to further the propaganda theme. For example, portions of Lincoln's Emancipation Proclamation and the Amnesty Declaration of 1863 were printed to support the Union cause and to undermine popular support for the Confederacy.[1]

Psychological warfare was used extensively in both world wars and in Vietnam, with billions of leaflets and radio broadcasts. By the start of World War I, most of the contemporary methods for leaflet dissemination had been developed. Mass propaganda techniques were used on a wide scale to send psychological messages to opposing forces. Lines were static in the WWI trenches, and that made target selection an easy task. Both sides used artillery shells, aircraft, balloons, and hand-held launchers to scatter leaflets—nearly 50 million leaflets by the end of the war from the Allied side alone. German forces complained about the Allied campaign, possibly because their own leaflet operations were fairly ineffective by comparison.[2]

During World War II, PSYWAR started slowly because of the lack of institutionalized psychological operations in the armies and because of the early defeats of France and other European countries. Germany used propaganda newspapers and public placards in its occupied territories as weapons against the resistance movements and to drum up opposition to the Jews.

Allied leaflet operations benefited from the introduction of the leaflet bomb, the only new PSYWAR technique developed during WWII. The Allies distributed billions of leaflets in Europe, Africa, and the Orient once psychological operations got under way. The Germans used the V-1 rocket to deliver leaflets to Britain. Most WWII leaflets were delivered by aircraft and artillery.[3]

The radio was also widely used by both sides in WWII. The Allies sent optimistic messages to the occupied countries that sometimes contained hidden instructions to the resistance. German radio used the British traitor William Joyce, known as Lord Haw Haw, to ridicule the Allied side. Joyce was hanged for treason after the armistice. Japan used an American-born Japanese woman to broadcast taunting messages, bad news from home, and music to American soldiers in the Pacific. "Tokyo Rose" was sentenced to prison after the surrender.[4]

Psychological warfare was intense in Vietnam. The 4th PSYOP Group, with four PSYOP battalions, conducted mass operations throughout the country, including leaflets, ground loudspeakers, airborne loudspeakers, civil operations, and press propaganda. Psychological warfare was also heavily used at the tactical level to support ongoing military combat operations. Units in the field had their own loudspeaker platoons to supply on-the-spot, tailored PSYWAR to support the immediate combat situation.

One of the main North Vietnamese PSYWAR instruments was Radio Hanoi, which broadcast patriotic music, propaganda messages, and appeals to the South Vietnamese people to support Vietcong forces acting in their countryside.

Civil actions were extensively used by the United States to counter Vietcong propaganda and to "pacify," or neutralize, Vietcong operating areas. Loudspeakers, newspapers, and leaflets were used to fight for the people's minds.

Recently the US Army used psychological warfare in its attempt to persuade Panamanian dictator Manuel Noriega to come out of his haven in Panama City and surrender. They played loud rock music, which Noriega hated, over loudspeakers in an attempt to fray his nerves and lower his resistance.

TYPES OF PSYWAR

Strategic

Psywar is often divided into three major applications: strategic, tactical, and consolidation. Strategic PSYWAR involves propaganda, deliberate lies, or stretching the truth to prejudice minds and international opinion against the opponent. It has long-range goals and is targeted outside the battle area as well as inside. It seeks to create dissension in the enemy's country and among its soldiers.

In strategic PSYWAR you may paint a word and photo picture of your forces as freedom fighters defending their farms and villages. Your soldiers are heroes, common folk who have taken up arms to defend their inalienable rights. You back your assertions with photos of bombed-out schools and wounded children. Even if you started the war, your strategic propaganda says you had no choice because the enemy was about to attack you.

Your enemy is painted as a big guy beating up the poor little guy, a world power using its limitless might illegally against accepted standards of international behavior. You claim his soldiers are professionals, murdering without a conscience. They slaughter civilians and drop germs and poison gas. They are planning to nuke you into oblivion. In short, no matter what the "truth" is, you are the oppressed good guy and the enemy is Satan, the image of death.

If you succeed in this, your opponent will come under more than just your artillery fire. He will be bombarded by questions based on the half-truths in your propaganda. His answers will be easy to state but impossible to prove, a no-win situation. These arguments work on your own people, too, so strategic PSYWAR can also be used internally.

During a war, radio, television, newsreels, and the press are the conduits of strategic PSYWAR. Even some commercial motion pictures can be considered strategic PSYWAR because of the attitudes and way of life that they portray. Political cartoons on posters and in newspapers are used to depict the opponent's forces as invaders—foreigners who are "not like us." Nations bombard each other with radio programs in the opponent's language, broadcasting appeals by prominent people from the other side who feel the war is unethical and should be stopped. Each side attempts to jam the programs, an indication of their effectiveness.

Prisoners of war are often coerced into making false claims against their own country. Sometimes, they even volunteer to "apologize" for participating in the war or for dropping bombs. Staged photo opportunities show bombed-out baby food factories and hospitals as evidence of the illegality of the opponent's tactics.

Tactical

Tactical PSYWAR, usually with leaflets and loudspeakers, is closely tied to the battlefield. It seeks an immediate effect

I was crawling slowly, carefully along the side
a ditch when it happened. A hot, sharp pain
rough my right thigh, so intense that it numb
turned me. I don't remember very clearly whe
ed out or not. But I knew I was wounded.

I stopped crawling and lay down near an
ho also appeared to have been hit. I don't kno
e lay there – it seemed an eternity – until th
creased in intensity, but I was cold and scare
am. Eventually the pain near us ceased and
little moved past us, going far down the b

After a while, a Chinese soldier came alo
he any *I am a* really began to
– I had always heard that were I ever to su
rain or Chinese troops, I should be very badly
obably shot by most American troops but this I
derstandingly. I guess those false rumors were
culated among us so that we would fight –
you can imagine what fear I had for my life.

learn about these new way of government, th
ay of life

— Henry C. Conac

This letter was written by a US prisoner of war and used by North Korea
for propaganda purposes.

against enemy forces and civilians under your control. Just before a bombing raid, you drop leaflets telling people and soldiers they should flee the area. After the raid, you say, "I told you so. Maybe next time you should leave." After a particularly heavy artillery attack, you lob in leaflet shells with surrender passes and set up loudspeakers telling the battered enemy soldiers that it's better to be in a prison camp than to take such a beating. Tactical PSYWAR is immediate and responsive to the battlefield commander's needs. It is designed to enhance the commander's plan, to weaken the enemy's resolve, and to take away any enemy advantage.

Consolidation

Consolidation PSYWAR is aimed at civilians, often after territory has been liberated. It is especially valuable shortly after liberation, before military or civil authorities can assume the functions of government. Linked to the function called civil actions, it attempts to convince people that they are better off under the new government. They are assured that roads will be repaired and that new schools and hospitals will be built. Your doctors and medics offer aid to local people to counter enemy PSYWAR that you are barbarians and hate the local people.

Consolidation PSYWAR tries to reinforce the image that your forces are on the right side, the ones civilians should support. A friendly populace won't be a guerrilla force in your rear echelon. This kind of PSYWAR often consists of newspapers and leaflets that offer assurances, aid, and information and that call for peace.

PSYWAR PLANNING

Planning for psychological warfare is often described as an art, not a science, because there are too many unknown factors to determine a definitive plan. Behavioral psychology is certainly at the core, as is cultural anthropology, but the final plan is

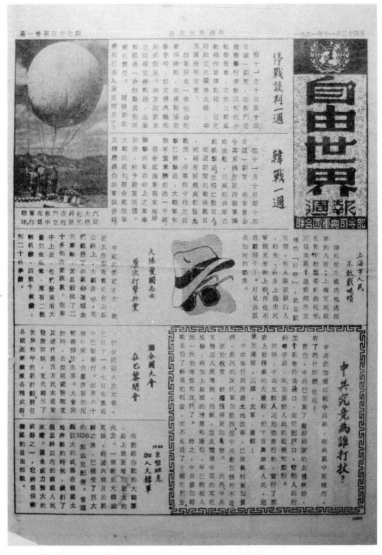

Printed by the 1st Radio Broadcasting and Leaflet Group and intended for civilians, this propaganda newspaper offered reliable news about the war and favorable comments about UN forces.

always tempered by the needs of the battle, the experience of the planners and executors, and the means available. A perfect PSYWAR plan can be defined as a clear objective against a defined target, conveyed in a credible and believable message, using the most appropriate means. In any PSYWAR plan, then, there are four interlocking factors: purpose, targeting, credibility, and means. What is the purpose of the PSYWAR operation? It cannot be an end in itself. It must reflect national policy. It should offer unique support to military operations and the commander in the field or the leader in the capital. This objective must be clear before the planning starts or it may not be met. What is the desired effect?

Targeting begins with a question: Who are we trying to influence? Targeting uses cultural anthropology—the science of how people live, what they believe, and how their culture responds—to try to determine everything that defines each culture in the target area. What is funny? What do the enemy soldiers joke about? What do they worry about? What do they value? What are their superstitions? How do they feel about the war and us? Other considerations are their food supply, health, national problems and stresses, graffiti, slang, taboos, and holidays. If their soldiers are draftees, you need to know how they feel about the war. What can you exploit so that your message meets your objective? This analysis is always incomplete and risky, especially under the time pressures and general confusion that surround every war. And it may indicate that a mass-media approach will not work because most nations are made up of multiple ethnic groups and they may not all respond to the same presentation or message.

Credibility is perhaps the toughest factor to achieve. If the propaganda asserts some fact, like the superiority of UN artillery, it must be independently verifiable by the target audience. The message must be believable, though not necessarily true. It must be simple and direct so that it can be understood

without much thought. If most of the enemy soldiers are conscripted farm boys who can't read, the simplest diagrams and
symbols must be used. The language and dialect must match
the audience. If humor is intended, the joke must be funny to
the guy in the foxhole. A drawing of an oppressive head of state
must be recognizable by the target. Lost credibility is disas-
trous and recovering believability takes precious time.

PSYWAR organizations often have review groups, with
cultural experts that screen operation plans before they are employed. Pretesting against a group of prisoners from the same
cultural group as the target can fine-tune a product before use,
especially if it is intended to be funny, increase fear, or elicit a
strong emotion.

The last factor in PSYWAR planning is means, the consideration of what tools, media, and methods are available to
convey the propaganda message to the target. Limitations may
force planners to use certain messages or delivery methods.
Radio broadcasts are of no use if your air force just blew up all
the enemy's power stations. With no electricity, there are no
working radios and therefore no receipt of the broadcast message; so don't bother planning one. In a few hours a battlefield
leaflet can be produced to respond to a developing tactical
situation. A loudspeaker mounted on a jeep might be the best
means to take immediate advantage of the enemy's misfortune.

EFFECTIVENESS

Judging the effectiveness of a PSYWAR operation is almost
impossible. The effect is often cumulative, achieving a surrender
after repeated efforts coordinated with several military attacks.
There usually is no immediate and observable link between the
cause (the PSYWAR) and effect. Careful interrogation of prisoners can help to gauge PSYWAR effectiveness. Did they see
leaflets? If so, did they surrender because of one? What did
they think of the leaflet, and was there punishment for picking
one up? Could they hear the loudspeaker? Did the searchlight

This leaflet used a heroic Korean figure to pose the question: "North Korea—Is Red China really a free country?"

bother their commander? After an area is liberated, interrogation of civilians may identify effects from PSYWAR operations, as may in-depth intelligence analysis. Did the factory shut down after the leaflets warned about the bombing raid? If loudspeakers claimed a particular unit was especially tough, did enemy commanders alter their troop movements? Analysis and testing help to improve the product and create the right message at the right time.

1. Carl Berger, *An Introduction to Wartime Leaflets* (Washington, DC: Special Operations Research Office, American University, 1959), p. 3.

2. Berger, *Wartime Leaflets*, pp. 3–4.

3. Berger, *Wartime Leaflets*, pp. 4–5.

4. Frederick G. Ruffner, Jr., and Robert C. Thomas, *Code Name Dictionary* (Detroit, MI: Grale Research, 1963).

5. Daniel C. Pollock, ed., *The Art and Science of Psychological Operations: Case Studies of Military Application* (US Army Pamphlet 525-7-1 and -2. Washington, DC: Government Printing Office, 1976), numerous references.

2

PSYWAR in the Korean War Era

Less than a day after President Harry Truman decided that the United States would send troops to Korea to aid the United Nations and South Korea against North Korea, the first propaganda leaflets were designed, printed, and dropped from an aircraft over the battle area. Less than twenty-four hours later, the first broadcasts were on the air to Korea from Radio Japan.

This rapid response had been made possible by a far-reaching decision in 1947 by the Far East Command to reestablish its Psychological Warfare Section (also termed a branch). Major General Charles Willoughby, the assistant chief of staff for intelligence, the G2, then appointed J. Woodall Greene, a former Army colonel who had conducted PSYWAR against the Japanese, to head it. One of his first actions was to set up a planning group to decide how the section could respond to any outbreak of hostilities in the Far Eastern theater. Greene scoured the Far East Command for former PSYWAR professionals and soon he gathered a small team. Even though there were only six people in the section at the start, their advanced planning meant that when the North Korean People's Army (NKPA) crossed the parallel, Far East Command was ready to respond. By the end of 1950, the section had expanded to more than thirty-five people. By 1952, it was transferred to the G3, Plans and Operations. Throughout the war, the Psychological Warfare Section (PWS) was also the coordinating agency for the PSYWAR activities of the United Nations.

THE OCPW
In 1950, after the North Korean invasion, President Truman established the Psychological Strategy Board (PSB) to form national policy for psychological warfare. This board planned overall PSYWAR operations and coordinated operations throughout the military. Wanting control of its own PSYWAR operations, the Army, on 15 January 1951, established what was to become one of the most important PSYWAR organizations, the Office of the Chief of Psychological Warfare, or the OCPW.

Established with some controversy, it held special staff status with direct access to the Army chief of staff. Its first chief, Brigadier General Robert McClure, had been General Dwight D. Eisenhower's chief of PSYWAR in Europe. The OCPW not only was responsible for PSYWAR operations in the Army as a whole, but it also conducted Cover and Deception as well as Unconventional Warfare, which grew into today's Special Forces. It provided the training, material, and doctrinal support for all psychological warfare units, including those in Korea.

McClure organized the Psychological Warfare Center at Fort Bragg, North Carolina, in April 1952. The center provided equipment and training in doctrine, tactics, and procedures for psychological warfare and the emerging field of special operations.[1]

The OCPW was organized into three divisions: Psychological Operations, Requirements, and Special Operations. The two operations divisions were further subdivided into branches on plans, operations, intelligence, and evaluation.

The Requirements Division was responsible for organizational issues, training, personnel, logistics, and research for the operations division.

The Secretary of the Army, Frank Pace, strongly endorsed psychological operations, stressing quality over quantity. The prevalent attitude of Army commanders in Korea had been to "bury the enemy in paper," but General Matthew Ridgway fully accepted Pace's position. Pace gave priority to tactical leaflet and loudspeaker operations because they offered direct support to the battlefield commander. He also sought to expand radio broadcasts, including stations strong enough to reach Chinese forces in Manchuria as well as in Korea.

To coordinate national PSYWAR policy, Pace relied on the Psychological Strategy Board in Washington. The Operations Research Office at Johns Hopkins University provided basic research and historical materials and references and analyzed PSYWAR operations. It was superseded by the Army's own Human Resources Research Office.

Much of the equipment available to support PSYWAR operations at the start of the Korean War was left over from World War II and was of doubtful reliability. General McClure expressed his concern and soon new equipment was under research and development, including a mobile leaflet printing plant, light and powerful loudspeakers for mobile use, and a 5,000-watt mobile radiobroadcasting unit. However, most analyses after the armistice showed that PSYWAR in Korea benefited little from this research. PSYWAR units were forced to fall back on methods developed during World War II. The effectiveness of these methods was stunted, however, because the Korean War was a different kind of war; there were vastly different political constraints and the enemy didn't play by western rules of warfare that underlie the Army's tactical warfare doctrine.

One of the few advances in PSYWAR in Korea was the realization that surrender was a sequential process. The enemy

soldier seldom decided to surrender on the spur of the mo-
ment. Instead, frustrations, fear of death, loneliness, homesick-
ness, and hatred for his leaders built up over time. PSYWAR
could provide the spark to get him thinking about quitting,
perhaps subconsciously at first. Then, in conjunction with a
terrible battle or artillery barrage to push him over the edge, a
surrender leaflet would give him the way out he needed. The
realization that surrender was a process influenced the PSY-
WAR campaign throughout the war.

The PSYWAR section of the Far East Command was the
hub of leaflet, radio, and loudspeaker activities throughout the
war in Korea. Satellite organizations were set up under the
Eighth Army and the X Corps to command tactical psychological warfare at the front. The Far East Air Force was the
main distributor of leaflets, and loudspeakers were attached to
two 21st TCS C-47s for use by the Eighth Army and X Corps
under the direction of the Fifth Air Force in Pusan. The section controlled strategic and tactical PSYWAR policy and the
deployment of tactical PSYWAR units in the battlefield. It set
up the Far East Command Printing and Publication Center to
design and print the millions of leaflets required during the
war. Radio activities used existing facilities in Japan to beam
messages to Korea.

PSYWAR and propaganda policy for leaflet, loudspeaker,
and radio operations followed three main military objectives:

1. Weaken the effectiveness and resistance of the North
Korean (and, later, the Communist Chinese) People's Army.

2. Bring the truth about the war to the people of North
Korea.

3. Bolster the morale of the South Korean troops and
civilian population.

The PSYWAR plan was set in Japan in weekly planning
sessions that involved PSYWAR and regional specialists as well
as Korean nationals. They studied the progress of the battle,

reviewed battle plans for the immediate future, examined intelligence gleaned from frontline interrogations of prisoners, and considered the availability of forces, the weather, and other factors. Using general policy guidelines, the radio and loudspeaker scripts and leaflet designs were drawn up. They were then approved by the policy board and sent into production.

Most of the leaflets used in Korea were designed under this process in the Tokyo Headquarters of the Psychological Warfare Section. Native Koreans were responsible for the final version of radio and loudspeaker scripts and for leaflet wording to ensure that the correct idiom was used. Leaflets were produced by the Printing and Publication Center in Yokohama, packaged in bundles and leaflet bombs, and sent daily by aircraft to Korea. Scripts were sent to tactical loudspeaker units and to broadcasting facilities in Japan and, later, Korea.

Four themes were stressed when planning PSYWAR operations against the North Koreans and Chinese troops:

1. Surrender and receive good food, humane treatment, medical care, and shelter from the dangers of war.

2. Surrender and you will stay alive to return to your home after UN forces win the war.

3. UN forces are superior in firepower. You cannot win.

4. A living North Korean patriot is better than a dead one.

Different themes were used on civilians, for consolidation efforts in recently liberated territory:

1. The Chinese and Korean Communists have conspired to make Korea a puppet state to make you a slave.

2. The Communists will exploit all of Korea for their own purposes.

3. The Communists lie when they preach peace and unity, and their actions reveal this truth.

4. All Koreans are brothers. The Communist war immorally pits them against one another.

5. The free nations of the world, through the United Nations, support the Republic of Korea against the Communist aggression.[2]

These themes were intended to subvert the morale of the North Korean army and the common Chinese soldier, who knew little about why he was fighting in Korea. Civilian themes were designed to thwart support to the North and to substantiate the validity of the South. They were aimed at bringing the truth to the Communist-led soldiers and the civilians under their control until they were liberated by UN forces and civil authorities could reestablish proper controls.

ARMY TACTICAL, STRATEGIC, AND CONSOLIDATION PSYWAR UNITS

At the close of World War II, operational PSYWAR units were disbanded along with much of the offensive military establishment. When the North Koreans crossed the 38th parallel in June 1950, the only operational PSYWAR unit was the small twenty-person Tactical Information Detachment at Fort Riley, Kansas.[3] It was expanded and sent to South Korea as the 1st Loudspeaker and Leaflet Company (1st L&L), arriving on 8 November 1950. It served as the Eighth Army's tactical PSYWAR operational focus in the Korean theater and, while it served the overall PSYWAR policies set in Tokyo, it took its orders from the tactical commanders responsible for the battle. Members often lived with the troops they supported, moving constantly as the front fluctuated. Loudspeakers were mounted on jeeps, tanks, and aircraft, and frontline leaflet production was established. As a tactical unit, the 1st L&L was called on to provide leaflet and loudspeaker scripts in very short order in direct support of combat operations, limited to a forty-mile zone north of the front lines.

The 1st L&L was organized in a Headquarters and three platoons: Propaganda, Publications, and Loudspeakers. The small Headquarters held the company leadership and its ad-

The front lines during the first phase of the war, ending with the UN forces isolated within the Pusan perimeter.

Steven Rook

ministrative staff. The Eighth Army Commander held close control over the 1st L&L by housing its Headquarters and Propaganda Platoon, which planned tactical PSYWAR operations, within his own Headquarters. The Publications Platoon designed and printed tactical leaflets, often more than three million leaflets each week, and the Loudspeaker Platoon manned the loudspeakers and wrote the scripts. Corps commanders at the front controlled their own loudspeaker sections deployed from the central Loudspeaker Platoon. Consolidation PSYWAR operations were conducted by the State Department's US Information Service. From Pusan, it ran programs over public address systems, printed newspapers and handouts, and made newsreels for dissemination to civilians under the jurisdiction of the Republic of Korea. It was the voice of reason during times of attack and panic and supplied reliable news of the war. Its members entered bombed-out cities and supplied education for children and other city services until South Korean civil authorities could take over.

For strategic PSYWAR operations, the 1st Radio Broadcasting and Leaflet Group (1st RB&L) was established at Fort Riley in April 1951 and sent to Korea in August. Its job was to support long-term objectives aimed at both the North and South Korean populaces as well as the Communist Chinese Forces and North Korean People's Army. When the 1st RB&L Group arrived in Japan in the summer of 1951, it assumed control over all strategic PSYWAR operations in Korea, although the PSYWAR section continued to provide overall direction.[4]

The 1st RB&L was organized into three companies: Headquarters, Reproduction, and Mobile Radio. The Headquarters Company held the group leadership and the administrative and supervisory personnel necessary for it to function. The Reproduction Company held the highly skilled printing personnel and their wide array of equipment. They produced millions of nontactical leaflets and newspapers, often in color and in very short order, as many as 20 million a week, for dis-

National Archives

A PSYWAR exercise at Fort Riley, Kansas, using a loudspeaker unit mounted on a jeep.

semination by artillery shells and aircraft. Strategic leaflet drops were prohibited within forty miles of the front, where tactical leaflet units operated.

The Mobile Radio Broadcasting Company was a direct descendant of the mobile radio companies of World War II and used some of the same equipment. It conducted broadcasts over the entire Korean theater, writing and producing pro-

Men of the 3rd Reproduction Company produce leaflets at the Far East Command Printing and Publications Center in Japan.

grams and augmenting existing equipment when it had been battle damaged. Upon its arrival in the Far East, the 1st RB&L assumed operation of the Voice of the UN Command (VUNC), a propaganda radio station in Japan that had begun broadcasting to Korea on 29 June 1950 as the Voice of General MacArthur's Headquarters. It was redesignated VUNC in July 1950 after MacArthur was named commander in chief of all UN forces in Korea. Originally organized under the G2 (Intelligence) Special Projects Branch, VUNC was reorganized on 17 June 1951 under the G3 (Operations) Psychological Warfare Section, which retained control over it when the 1st RB&L took over its operation.

These units were hastily manned by reserve officers with backgrounds in journalism, newspaper printing, novel and script writing, art, and radio technology. They were given training in PSYWAR techniques at the Psychological Warfare School at Fort Riley where they learned basic PSYWAR prin-

ciples, strategic intelligence fundamentals, PSYWAR operations methods, and insights into the organization of foreign
military forces. But when these units arrived in Japan in August
1951, they were still inexperienced in the aspects of PSYWAR.
The training they received in Korean customs, language, and
social details was also inadequate for the job. The early emphasis was on quantity, not quality. Later, Korean nationals helped
in the design and targeting of their materials. By 1952, the 1st
RB&L could produce leaflets in sixteen languages and dialects.
Army, Air Force, and Navy officers were all trained at the
Psychological Warfare School at Fort Riley. Training was also
offered to students from Great Britain, Denmark, Norway,
Canada, France, Italy, and Belgium.

By 1953, a fourth company for consolidation PSYWAR
was added for operations in the areas under military authority.

AIR FORCE PSYWAR UNITS

When the North Koreans crossed the 38th parallel, there were
no PSYWAR units in the US Air Force, much less in the
Korean theater. The only airlift unit in the Far East was the
374th Troop Carrier Wing (Combat Cargo) of the 315th Air
Division stationed at Tachikawa Air Base near Tokyo. The missions of the 315th and its subordinate units were to provide
airlift to the Far East Command in nine "phases": airborne
assault, airdrop resupply, air-landed resupply, medical evacuation, airlift of entire units, aircrew training, air terminal system
operation, a system of daily scheduled flights in the Far East,
and Special Air Missions (SAM). PSYWAR was part of the
SAM phase, often performed in conjunction with other phases.

The 374th was the hub of military airlift in the Far East.
There was little traffic to Korea before the war, but during its
first year in combat, September 1950 to September 1951, the
315th Air Division air-dropped more than 20,000 personnel
and 17,000 tons of supplies, air-landed another 284,000 tons of
supplies, carried more than 641,000 passengers, evacuated

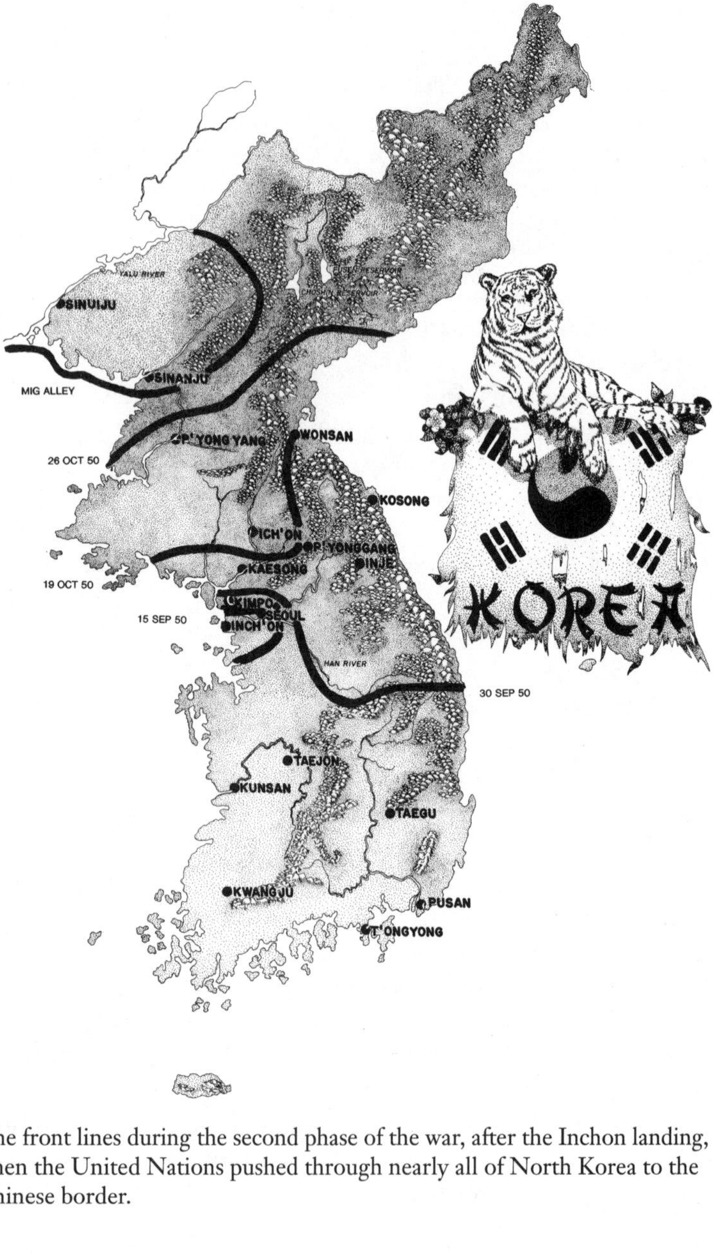

Map labels:

YALU RIVER
SINUIJU
SINANJU
MIG ALLEY
P'YONG YANG
WONSAN
26 OCT 50
KOSONG
ICH'ON
P'YONGGANG
INJE
KAESONG
19 OCT 50
KIMPO
SEOUL
INCH'ON
15 SEP 50
HAN RIVER
30 SEP 50
TAEJON
KUNSAN
TAEGU
KWANGJU
PUSAN
T'ONGYONG

KOREA

Steven Rook

The front lines during the second phase of the war, after the Inchon landing, when the United Nations pushed through nearly all of North Korea to the Chinese border.

161,000 patients, and flew 83,572 sorties with 248,029 hours in the air.[5]

The day after President Truman declared that he would send US forces to support the United Nations and South Korea, the 374th's commander, Colonel Swampy Crawford, dispatched his C-54s to Korea to evacuate diplomats, missionaries, and other civilians from Seoul and later from Taejon to Japan. There were few US troops to extract. Less than twenty-four hours after Truman's declaration, Colonel Crawford ordered the first PSYWAR operation of the war. It was flown by Captain Howard Secor in his 374th C-46. He first carried cargo from Tachikawa to the Army at Ashiya, Japan. There he reloaded with hastily printed leaflets and flew to Korea, passing low over the rapidly advancing North Korean People's Army and the former South Korean cities and territory they now occupied and dropping leaflets. The leaflets urged civilians to remain calm, telling them that US forces would soon join them to throw the invaders out.

Secor flew his C-46 at 500 feet and less to drop his leaflets, an eight-hour mission that often risked fire from the North Korean troops despite his occasional fighter escort. His crew dropped thousands of leaflets over Seoul, Taejon, and several other cities that were already under the control of the North. The main message of the leaflets was to convince the North Koreans that the United States and extensive UN forces from around the world were on their way to help South Korea defend itself. Faced with this surge of help, the North Koreans would ultimately lose. There were no surrender leaflets. The victorious NKPA troops weren't interested in surrender at this time.

Other units flying C-119 (314th Troop Carrier Group) and C-46 (437th Troop Carrier Wing) aircraft also performed propaganda, leaflet, and airdrop missions. In late 1951, control over Air Force PSYWAR operations was centralized under the Fifth Air Force at Taejon.

National Air and Space Museum

The 21st TCS aircrew attempts to toss leaflets from the open door of a C-47. Early in the war, leaflets were carried in bundles that were opened at the door and many blew back in.

One of the most famous airlift units of the war was attached to the 347th: the 21st Troop Carrier Squadron, the Kyushu Gypsies.[6] The 21st was attached to the 374th Troop Carrier Wing and upward to the 315th Air Division (Combat Cargo). Later in the war, the squadron was transferred to the Fifth Air Force. After Truman's declaration, they were immediately transferred from Clark Field in the Philippines to Ashiya, Japan. Their four-engine C-54s were consolidated with the 6th and 22nd Troop Carrier Squadrons of the 374th. The 21st was refitted with twin-engine C-47s, and every twin-engine-qualified pilot Colonel Crawford could find was reassigned to the 21st. From its base at Ashiya, the 21st was just across the Sea of Japan from Korea.

Soon they were joined at Ashiya by C-119, air rescue, and

fighter units. As Ashiya filled up, the 21st was moved to Brady Field, a bare airfield with no amenities, but one close to the more comfortable living facilities at Camp Hakata. The squadron was to make many more moves before the war was over. "We're just a bunch of Gypsies!" members would say. The nickname stuck and they became the "Kyushu Gypsies." (Kyushu is the name of a large island in Japan.) Because of the excellent short-field capacity and the ruggedness of its C-47s, the 21st always got the toughest air resupply and transportation missions of the war. It landed on island beaches, carried supplies to the Marines when they were surrounded by the Chinese at Chosin and evacuated their wounded, and carried supplies into temporary airfields scraped out of the rocky Korean soil, often under fire.

The SAM detachment of the 21st was heavily involved in VIP transport as well as leaflet, loudspeaker, and agent missions during the war. Later, when airfields became available at Taegu and Kimpo, the Gypsies were transferred to Korea and flew an old B-17 on special classified missions, a VC-47 that carried distinguished people such as the president of South Korea, Syngman Rhee, and John J. Muccio and Ellis O. Briggs, US ambassadors, and loudspeaker-equipped C-47s called "the Voice." The 21st was later joined by C-47s from Greece and Thailand, making it the only three-nation unit in Korea.

The 21st's pilots were on "indefinite" temporary duty when in Korea and their stay was determined by the number of missions they flew. Because the 21st always worked closely with tactical units close to the front, their missions usually had short flying times—well under two hours—and crews could fly several missions each day, sometimes as many as five or six. Therefore, tours in Korea for Gypsy pilots were generally only ninety days.

Late in 1951, the Gypsies and their combat cargo and SAM detachments were transferred to the Fifth Air Force. Leaflet operations gradually were transferred from the C-47s

The 21st TCS aircrew "kicking" leaflet bundles from a C-47 later in the war. These bundles were opened by blasting caps with delayed fuses.

to larger aircraft, and the Gypsies turned to special missions such as landing on beaches and in narrow valleys, though combat cargo aircraft continued to bring in leaflet bundles and bombs from the central printing plants in Japan.

Another unit performing Air Force PSYWAR was the 581st Air Resupply and Communications (ARC) Wing, flying fixed-wing aircraft and helicopters.[7] A PSYWAR unit independent from regular Army operations, the 581st printed millions of leaflets in its own Printing Squadron, interrogated prisoners in its Holding and Briefing Squadron, and performed communications intercepts in its Communications Squadron. It also used balloons to deliver leaflets. Its sister wing, the 582nd, whose personnel were often used in Korea, was stationed in Libya. Well-known ARC alumni include legendary pilots

The front lines during the third and last phase of the war, when the lines stagnated along the 38th parallel.

Colonel Fish and Killer Kane and William Peter Blatty, then an Arabic linguist with the 582nd, now known as the author of *The Exorcist.*

Operating from Clark Field in the Philippines, the 581st provided support to the CIA for agent drops and their extraction or resupply, aerial resupply of Korean guerrilla bands, support of commando operations, and other covert missions, in addition to its routine leaflet drops. SA-16 flying boats and H-19 helicopters of the 581st were often loaned to support air rescue operations. Eventually, as Air Force units received new planes, the CIA gained control of older C-46s and C-47s for its own air operations.

The PSYWAR organizations and their functions, which were established during the war, continue to this day, though unit names have changed.

1. For a complete discussion of the OCPW and its relationship to the development of US Army Special Operations, including PSYWAR, see Alfred H. Paddock, Jr., *US Army Special Warfare: Its Origins, Psychological and Unconventional Warfare, 1941–1952* (Washington, DC: National Defense University Press, 1982).

2. These statements about objectives and themes are from "Psychological Warfare in Korea, An Interim Report," in *Public Opinion Quarterly,* spring 1951. It is the best concise summary of PSYWAR in Korea and possibly the only one to discuss the themes and objectives of the overall Korean War PSYWAR campaign.

3. Paddock, *US Army Special Warfare,* p. 94.

4. The 1st L&L and 1st RB&L are seldom discussed in Korean War histories, though they were the pivotal organizations in the PSYWAR campaign. The appendix to Paul Linebarger's book, *Psychological Warfare* (Washington, DC: Infantry Journal Press, 1948, 1954) is one of the few references that discuss these organizations and

their structure. Two others are Paddock, *US Army Special Warfare*, and Frank R. Barnett and Carnes Lord, eds., *Political Warfare and Psychological Operations: Rethinking the US Approach* (Washington, DC: National Defense University Press, 1989).

5. These figures are from *Flexible Air Transport*, an obscure booklet published 15 November 1951 by the Headquarters of the 315th Air Division (Combat Cargo). It includes many rare photos and details on the organization of combat cargo in Korea. It is hard to find; I found my copy in the US Air Force Academy library.

6. Nearly all the information of the Kyushu Gypsies in this book was gleaned from the rare (although the USAFA library has several copies) unit history of the 315th by Captain Annis G. Thompson, *The Greatest Airlift: The Story of Combat Cargo* (Tokyo: 315 Air Division, May 1954). The photos and personal details are not to be found anywhere else. Many details of the Gypsies came from veterans of that detachment.

7. Apparently, the 581st was quite secretive; there are few details. I am indebted to Bill Klopp, a pilot who flew with the 581st, for much of the information on this unit.

PART TWO

Lies, Leaflets, and Loudspeakers

Leaflets, radio and press propaganda, and loudspeakers on aircraft and vehicles were the major PSYWAR activities during the Korean War. Dry, static reports reveal what was done, what the numbers were, and who did what and when. To convey the true-to-life story, however, these facts are interwoven here with the stories of those who carried out PSYWAR, the pilots of the Kyushu Gypsies, soldiers of the Eighth Army, men of the 1st Marine Division, and others.

3

Leaflets

The method most widely used in waging PSYWAR during the Korean War was through leaflets. UN forces delivered more than two billion leaflets on North Korea and North Korean forces from 1950 to 1953. At peak production more than twenty million leaflets were produced per week. Some estimated that more than 100,000 North Korean and Chinese soldiers surrendered as a result of US PSYWAR activities.[1]

Leaflets were printed advertisements that ranged in size from three by five inches to the size of a newspaper. They were delivered most often by aircraft in a special bomb with a hinged side that blew off after a predetermined amount of time.

The bomb was known as the M16-A1 Cluster Adapter of World War II origin. It held 45,000 four-by-five-inch leaflets or 22,500 five-by-eight-inch leaflets and weighed more than 170 pounds when fully loaded. It was dropped by B-26s, B-29s, and probably by the T-6. (There's a photo of a T-6 dropping leaflets, but no mention of this in official records.) The B-29 carried thirty-two such bombs, releasing 1,440,000 leaflets in one load! The bomb carried a time delay separation charge. After release at 15,000 to 25,000 feet, the bomb halves separated at 1,000 to 2,000 feet to concentrate the leaflets over a specific target area.[2]

Korean civilians load newspaper leaflets into a bomb in Seoul in September 1952.

Aircrew from the Kyushu Gypsies tries to throw leaflets from a C-47.

Leaflets were also dropped in huge reels like overgrown rolls of theater tickets, and in bundles that looked like hay bales, a Korean War development. Early in the war, the bundles were opened in the aircraft and the leaflets dumped out by hand. Gusts of wind often blew them back into the planes. Later, blasting caps with delay fuses were fixed to the bundles so they could be thrown out intact, to be popped open clear of the cargo door.

Leaflets were also delivered by special artillery shells and by hand. The 105mm howitzer shell held 400 four-by-five-inch leaflets. Usually, an empty smoke shell was used; smoke shells were easily modified in the field into leaflet carriers. The range of the gun limited its use to an area close to the front lines, but it could deliver leaflets with precision and in any weather. This delivery method was easy for local PSYWAR or intelligence personnel to use. They could print their own

National Air and Space Museum

Airman sets the timing cap on a leaflet bundle prior to release.

Captain Kleckner hands propaganda leaflets printed by the 1st Loudspeaker and Leaflet Company, PSYWAR Section, to Lieutenant Ackley, as he prepares to take off for a flight over enemy territory in his L-19 observation aircraft, June 1952.

leaflets and respond rapidly to a tactical situation. Leaflet shells could also be combined with high-explosive shells to augment offensive combat actions. Experience and POW interrogation showed that the leaflet shell was especially effective when used before and after heavy artillery barrages.

The PSYWAR message was aimed at the ordinary North Korean or Chinese soldier and at the common people in North Korean–controlled territory. More than 30 percent of the surrendering soldiers were functionally illiterate, able to read only road signs and the simplest instructions. Most of the rest read only marginally better, so UN PSYWAR leaflets used simple phrases, supported by symbols, photos, and cartoons. Tactical surrender leaflets provided a simple map showing the easiest

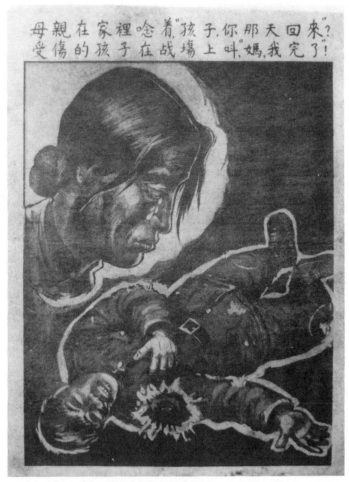

母親在家裡唸着"孩子,你那天回來?
受傷的孩子在战場上叫"媽,我完了!"

The message of this UN leaflet is that the Chinese soldier's wife or mother will weep when he dies on the battlefield.

route to UN lines. All they had to do was avoid getting shot by their own troops.

UN leaflets often played on Korean prejudices against the Chinese and Soviets, reinforced low North Korean morale by

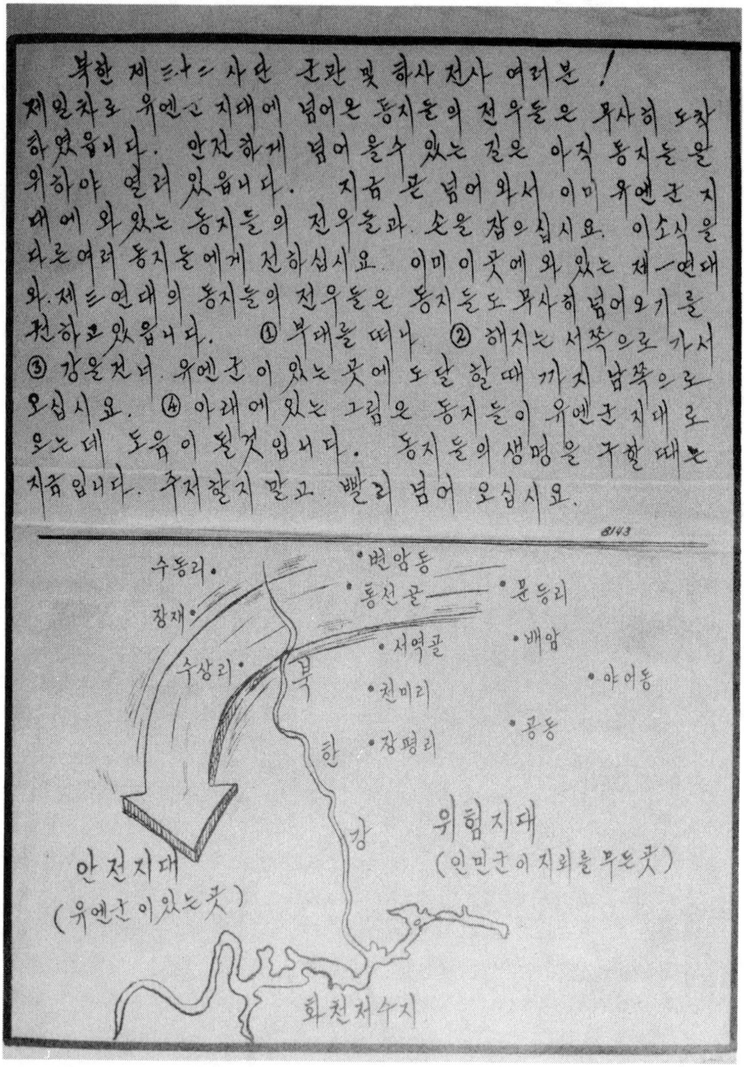

북한 제三十二 사단 군관 및 하사 전사 여러분!
제일차로 유엔군 지대에 넘어온 동지들의 전우들은 무사히 도착
하였읍니다. 안전하게 넘어 올수 있는 길은 아직 동지들을
위하야 열려 있읍니다. 지금 곧 넘어 와서 이미 유엔군 지
대에 와 있는 동지들의 전우들과 손을 잡으십시요. 이소식을
다른 여러 동지들에게 전하십시요. 이미 이곳에 와 있는 제一연대
와.제二연대의 동지들의 전우들은 동지들도 무사히 넘어오기를
전하고 있읍니다. ① 부대를 떠나 ② 해지는 서쪽으로 가서
③ 강을건너. 유엔군이 있는 곳에 도달 할 때 까지 남쪽으로
오십시요. ④ 아래에 있는 그림은 동지들이 유엔군 지대로
오는데 도움이 될것입니다. 동지들의 생명을 구할 때는
지금입니다. 주저하지 말고 빨리 넘어 오십시요.

수등리 ·
장재 ·
수상리 ·
· 편암등
· 통신골 ── · 문등리
· 서역골 · 배암
· 천미리 · 아어동
· 장평리 · 콩동

위험지대
(인민군이 지휘를 무는곳)

안전지대
(유엔군이있는곳)

화천저수지

8143

This surrender leaflet, prepared for the North Korean 32nd Division, directs soldiers to freedom. It tells them to leave their unit, walk toward the setting sun, swim across the river, and then go south until they find UN units. "Do not hesitate! Tomorrow may be too late! Save your life now!"

reminding them that they were being brutally treated by their officers, and focused on Korean or Chinese beliefs in ghosts, demons, angry gods, and fate. Defecting NKPA soldiers told their interrogators about their poor training, bad or missing equipment, the lack of ammunition, frostbite, and lack of food and medical care. Leaflets echoed these themes to the NKPA soldiers in the field. They worked on every man's fear of death or injury, his worry over his family, and the possibility that he would never see them again.

The leaflets were intended to create doubt in the NKPA soldiers as to his leaders' abilities and his personal place in the war. They tried to invoke nostalgia with traditional Korean themes of family and way of life. They had to be carefully written with a clear idea of the audience's literacy, fears, and opinions. They had to convey the right message and make the right suggestion to the right guy at the right time. One leaflet might carry a message in Korean, Chinese, and Russian, and semantic choices and translations in all three languages were critical. A phrase that worked in English might not make sense in Chinese, or it might even be funny or absurd, sending the wrong message. Some UN leaflets apparently were so effective that the Chinese just translated the message into English and dropped them on UN troops. It might take weeks or months and a series of leaflets before the impact of the message would take effect, but gradually, the enemy soldier might fight less bravely, be sick more often, be unwilling to do anything beyond what he was required to do, slow down, or perhaps finally desert.

Leaflets were printed in black ink with occasional strong reds and blues. Photos were used for special purposes, as evidence of atrocities committed or of the UN's beneficent treatment of POWs. The PSYWAR message was intended for a particular time and set of circumstances. It might not be appropriate a month later; therefore, most leaflets were printed on

Aimed at the 2nd Division of the NKPA, this UN leaflet says, "Please stay alive so we can build a new country. Learn from the story of this soldier's letter." The letter describes how the soldier was wounded and how he used a surrender pass to go to the UN side while on sentry duty. He left at 2 A.M. and found safety in UN custody. He tells his buddies to pick up the passes that fall from the sky and follow his example.

soft and degradable paper so that they disintegrated quickly. Safe conduct passes and surrender leaflets were printed on much better paper so that they could be carried in a pocket or shoe for months.

Leaflets were also targeted at civilians in NKPA-controlled territory. They depicted the NKPA soldier as crude and brutal, a puppet of the Soviets or Chinese. They depicted Soviet advisers as a privileged class, using race prejudice to undermine their acceptance by the populace. Working on rumors, national prejudices, and simple logic, they sought to weaken the support given to the NKPA troops and to solicit protection for downed UN pilots or soldiers separated from their units.

One of the more successful leaflet themes took advantage of the mutual mistrust between the Soviets and Chinese. At the time of the Korean War, Mao Tse-tung and Joseph Stalin were competing for world Communist leadership and Korea merely provided an arena for their contest. Initially, the war offered the Soviets a way to test their post–World War II strength, but soon the inability of the NKPA to hold off UN forces led them

A UN leaflet implies that medical aid will be immediately offered to the Chinese soldier when he surrenders.

This UN leaflet suggests to Chinese and North Korean soldiers that they are being pushed into the conflict by the Soviet Union.

to consider other areas of the world. Stalin took his time in supplying the Koreans and insisted that the Chinese pay cash for their war materials. Many UN leaflets played on the theme that the Chinese were sacrificing their lives to benefit the Soviets or that North Korea was merely the last pawn in a Soviet and Chinese political chess game.

Early PSYWAR during the rapid North Korean push southward was intended for South Koreans, telling them to hold on. The first leaflet aimed at Communist forces was produced seven weeks into the war. Early in the war, nearly one third of Communist POWs said they had been influenced by UN PSYWAR—usually leaflets—in their decision to surrender. Later, the figure was lowered because researchers determined many POWs were eager to please and merely told interrogators what they wanted to hear. Later in the war, this percentage genuinely went up as UN PSYWAR became focused on Communist forces.

TYPES OF LEAFLETS

Research after the war by the Special Operations Research Office classified leaflets into three types: directive, informative, and persuasive.[3] The first two leaflets are useful in strategic, tactical, and consolidation operations; the persuasive leaflet is used only for strategic and tactical situations. Directive leaflets gave orders to the target audience. The PLAN STRIKE leaflets that warned people in bombing target areas were of this type. The leaflets told the North Koreans near the targets to leave their homes and the factories to escape the death and destruction of the bomber attack. The surrender pass often told the Communist soldier where to go to surrender and how to make his way through the lines to safety. The informative leaflet had tried to tell the audience the truth. In Korea, one informative leaflet told the Communist soldier that his air force had been destroyed. It was easy for the soldier to confirm; he seldom, if ever, saw any Communist aircraft. In effect, his air force had been destroyed and UN planes flew without opposition. His sky was filled with UN aircraft. The persuasive leaflet tried to persuade the target to take a certain action or to change his mind. Surrender leaflets sometimes took this form. They presented the logical argument that surrendering was preferable to dying.

The newspaper leaflet was one of the most effective informative leaflets. Reliable news was hard to come by in the war zone and a credible newspaper leaflet was welcome on both sides of the lines. The United Nations produced at least five newspaper leaflets: *Parachute News, Free World News, Free World Weekly Digest, Free Korea,* and *Rehabilitation News.*[4] A small news sheet aimed at the mountain guerrillas was also produced. North Korea produced *Peace,* a compilation of negative articles cut from US newspapers, and *Democratic Korea.* The news

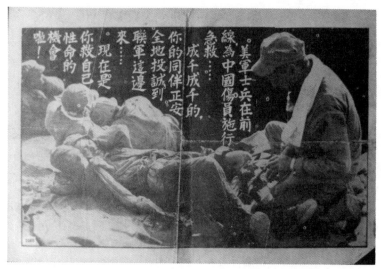

According to this UN leaflet, a Chinese soldier who surrenders will be treated by a UN medic.

sheets had to present news of interest to the target audience without overt propaganda. News leaflets also were designed for one-time use to comment on special events.

HOW LEAFLETS WERE PRODUCED

The sequence of annotated photographs in this chapter was taken by the US Army in 1953 to demonstrate to the public how leaflets were produced. The photos were used in exhibits and posters but have seldom, if ever, been published in an open source document.

Most of the leaflets used during the war were designed by the Psychological Warfare Branch in Japan. The theme was selected by the staff in response to a particular objective, and the art department drew the leaflet. The text was written in English by the PWB staff and then translated into Korean, Chinese, and Russian by the resident translators. The printing and packaging were done at the printing center in Yokohama and then airlifted to Korea, just a few hours away by combat cargo aircraft.

KYUSHU GYPSIES

The Kyushu Gypsies were the workhorses of airborne leaflet operations, especially early in the war. Always moving as the front shuttled up and down the Korean Peninsula, the Gypsies lived in tents and never had permanent facilities. Because of their resourcefulness, their camps always had hot showers made with fifty-five-gallon drums, a bar (the Auger Inn), cabinets for personal items, and decorations that belied their transitory existence.

The Gypsies compiled an exceptional record. They were involved in many dangerous cargo missions, such as the BEACHCOMBER operation, when they landed on beaches at low tide to resupply the Cho-do Island air rescue and radar installation. Most Gypsy missions were into UN-controlled ter-

National Archives

The text section of the 1st Radio Broadcasting and Leaflet Group compiled Korean and Chinese texts for UN leaflets. Tokyo, April 1952.

ritory or in areas fairly close to the battle lines. Gypsy pilots
sometimes were given missions to resupply special forces units
and guerrilla bands deep in enemy territory. They even made
some unofficial visits to Communist China.

MARC MICHALAKES, 21st TCS—For the winter
'50–'51, I was based at K-14, Kimpo, and for the spring
and summer of '51 at K-37, Taegu. We flew leaflet,
agent drop, radio intercept, day-recce [reconnais-
sance], and loudspeaker day/night. The commander
during my tenure was Captain Henry C. Aderholt, who
retired as a brigadier general.

When I arrived in the Far East in November '49,
the only troop carrier wing was at Tachikawa Air Base
near Tokyo. The 6th and 22nd squadrons were at
Tachikawa and the 21st was at Clark Field, Philippines.
When the Korean War started, the 21st was moved to
Ashiya Air Base on Kyushu Island as an augmented
C-47 squadron to resupply the forces in Korea. The
C-47 was the only STOL (short takeoff and landing)
type in the theater. Korean airfields were poor and
many were unusable for the C-54 of the 374th TC
Wing. The 21st TCS flew round-the-clock, three
shifts to resupply, airdrops, air land, air evac, et cetera,
until the C-119s arrived from the states in the fall of
1950. I went to PSYWAR first in December 1950 and
flew eighty-six missions, all behind the lines, not including the combat cargo flights of resupply, airdrop,
and air evac of wounded.

The Special Air Missions detachment of the Gypsies was
responsible for leaflet and loudspeaker operations. The pilots
and aircrews planned each mission according to the require-

Sergeants Hal Weed and John Davenport prepare material in the graphic arts section of the 1st Radio Broadcasting and Leaflet Group, Tokyo, April 1951.

National Archives

Master Sergeant John Ham operates the process copy camera at the FEC Printing and Publications Center, Japan, April 1952.

ments of the UN command. Friendly antiaircraft and artillery units were notified of their flight plan so they could limit their fire. UN troops in the area that was to be papered were also notified, especially if surrender leaflets were to be dropped. Most of the leaflet drops were made from the loudspeaker-equipped Voice aircraft to which Korean men and women were assigned in order to broadcast to North Korean and Chinese troops via the loudspeaker unit. During a mission, the Voice would also broadcast to the US lines so that the troops knew they should expect prisoners and would not fire on the surrendering Communists.

Early in the war, most missions were flown during the day so that the leaflets would be picked up right away. The loudspeakers would simultaneously blare, "Surrender or die! Fight on and you will be killed! Surrender and you can get good food, medical care, and comfortable quarters!"[5]

The leaflets were specific on how to surrender. Cartoons

showed the Communist soldiers what to do and simple maps of the immediate area showed them where to go. They were encouraged to surrender in groups after first destroying their rifles. One leaflet guaranteed safe passage to any number of soldiers.

The loudspeaker flights were especially dangerous. The loudspeakers, powerful though they were, were not strong enough to be heard over the roar of the engines unless the air-

National Archives

At the FEC Printing and Publications Center, a soldier operates a Harris LTV press as he prepares leaflets for the 1st RB&L, April 1952.

The press operator and the chief of the FEC printing plant inspect sheets of five-by-eight-inch leaflets as they roll off the press in Yokohama, Japan, November 1950. The leaflet brags about the UN front lines being close to the Chinese border, but within a few weeks, the Chinese army had forced UN forces far southward.

plane flew very low, perhaps 300 to 400 feet. It was not unusual for a Gypsy C-47 to actually fly below the level of enemy soldiers occupying hills around UN positions. This made them easy targets and the Voice planes constantly suffered bullet holes and wounded aircrew from ground fire. There was another hazard for the low-flying planes: The Communists strung steel cables across narrow valleys in hopes of snaring a Voice plane or other aircraft that might be flying low after a takeoff from the valley floor. Several C-47 and C-46 combat cargo aircraft and a few fighters were destroyed this way.

Because of the dangers in flying low and slow during the day, the 315th commander changed the mission time to later in the day and at a higher altitude or at night. This caused a dilemma for the pilots, who knew that they needed to fly low for the loudspeakers to be heard. They compromised by flying only slightly higher during day missions only. The biggest PSYWAR operation early in the war was conducted with the Munsan paratroop drop of the 187th Regimental Combat Team (RCT). The troops were dropped by 315th C-46s and C-119s. At the same time, four SAM C-47s dropped surrender leaflets from a low altitude in support of the operation. The leaflets pointed to the massive show of force and urged Communist soldiers to surrender. Records show that 127 soldiers surrendered as a result, each carrying a safe conduct pass. SAM aircraft flew as often as six times per day for seven days in support of the Munsan operation.

During the mission, one C-119 was badly hit and the crew bailed out. They were spotted by a Voice that circled their position and talked to them via the loudspeaker system to determine their health and status. Those on the ground used the cloth panels from their survival kits to answer yes and no. The Voice circled for three hours until a rescue helicopter arrived.

One mission stands out. During a murderous artillery and mortar barrage on Chinese positions in May 1951, a SAM aircraft spotted a group of 1,800 Chinese soldiers. The Voice began to drop leaflets and started to broadcast, "Life or death—it is your choice." The timing was right. The troops were thoroughly battered and eager to find an escape. The Voice directed them to UN lines after alerting the UN troops to be prepared to accept 1,800 surrendering Chinese. The Chinese troops surrendered, leaving behind their weapons but bringing with them their pack horses and mules.

Late in the war, the SAM detachment, then under Major Harry Aderholt, was transferred to the Fifth Air Force, becoming the 6461st. Much of the leaflet mission was parceled out to other units, such as the 581st Air Resupply and Communications Wing.

ROY DUNHAM, 21st TCS/6th TCS—I was with the 21st when they were in the Philippines at Clark AFB. I was transferred to a sister squadron, the 6th Troop Carrier Squadron, the C-54, "Bully Beef Express." We were told it was just a TDY; don't take all your belongings. I've never been back to the PI again! It was well known if you screwed up, you could be transferred to the 21st as punishment. Most of us didn't prefer to live out of our duffel bags, so we tried to stay clean. A couple of our guys taxied a C-54 into another C-54 one night almost head-on. Both of the damaged wings had to be changed. If my memory serves me right, one or both of the guys were transferred to the 21st instead of [getting] a court-martial.

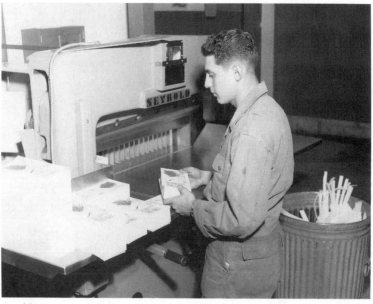

A soldier operates the paper cutter at the FEC printing plant, April 1952.

MARC MICHALAKES, 21st TCS—We first and second lieutenants needed to poke fun at the constant movements of the 21st from one air base after another. We called our squadron the Finger in the Ring Squadron. No base wanted us for long.

DICK HUGHES, 21st TCS—The South Korean chief of police would recruit people in Taegu to parachute into North Korea and then walk back to the South and report what they had seen. We gave them one practice jump at night and then took them up north and dropped them out at night at 1,000 feet. Also dropped teams of two or three men at night into North Korea. We would try to establish radio contact with them later.

The 21st TCS aircraft were about the only night flyers during the early days of the war. The enemy thought by the sound of our engines [cargo planes] that we were harmless, so they would not bother to put out their campfires at night when we flew over. We took a C-47, borrowed a bomb shackle from a fighter group, and mounted a napalm tank on it. Wasn't very accurate but could hit close enough that they [the enemy] would put out the campfires and maybe freeze the rest of the night. Korean winters were very, very cold.

The most exciting mission I flew was a propaganda leaflet drop behind the Chinese lines. This was when the front line was at the Han River and the city of Seoul was enemy-held territory. We were flying low over Seoul, dropping surrender leaflets where we thought it would do some good. Whenever we saw some enemy troops, we would sweep down and bombard them with invitations to surrender. Some of them didn't like it and started shooting at us. The right engine was shot out, the rudder cable severed, the hydraulic system shot up. We were able to glide across the Han River and belly into the UN side. Leaflets were scattered everywhere. The plane was stripped, even though they were close enough to catch enemy fire. Tech orders were burned, instruments removed. Before the Chinese took over that area, the Marines thoroughly burned what we left of the plane. One of the pilots flying with us was James Doolittle, Jimmy's son.

MARION WILLIAMS, 21st TCS—In hindsight, I do believe our people knew the war was coming. Several weeks before 25 June, I took a C-54 from the Philippines to the States for overhaul. On the way to the States, everything was normal. Coming back a week later with replacement planes, at Guam's north airfield, now called Anderson, the antiaircraft guns were already in place and revetments were being put up to protect the B-29s. Up until this time, I had been flying routine passenger runs, even though we were a troop carrier squadron. We suddenly started flying formations and dropping material for practice. Everyone was given a position to man in an emergency.

Our first mission was flying the 25th Infantry from Japan to Korea. There weren't any fields, so we used the old Japanese ones. They hadn't been used since World War II and rice had been planted to the edge of the runways. As we taxied down with the C-54s, the runways acted like Jell-O. We landed one way, unloaded, turned, and took off in the opposite direction as the other planes circled overhead, waiting to land.

There was a lot of tension at that time. I was co-pilot for the squadron commander. He got out of the seat and went back to expedite the unloading. All of a sudden, he came running up, got on the radio, and told the other planes to scatter; there was a formation of MIGs coming in. The MIGs landed in the rice next to the runway and started eating lunch. They were just birds, but they did fly a beautiful formation! I don't think any of us ever mentioned the bird bit to the colonel.

Our C-54s were taken away and we were given C-47s. It was a wonderful plane to fly. We would leave Japan loaded with supplies and then go wherever they needed us, as long as the gas held out. At the time of the Pusan Perimeter [an early phase of the war], our main job was dropping supplies to cut-off units; they seemed to be everywhere. The last planes into the airfields stayed in case they were overrun so we could carry out the wounded. I spent a lot of nights [sleeping] on a stretcher under the plane. We had a few missions to drop leaflets, but most of the time we carried a few bundles to drop after our main job was done.

The North Koreans started getting better at leading [aiming ahead of a moving target] the planes. At first, my plane got a few holes in the tail, but as the war went on, the holes moved up the plane. We mostly lost planes to weather and poor navigation aids. We dropped leaflets, cargo, and troops out the side cargo doors, which were removed most of the time. In the beginning of the war, things were very fluid. Once we were sent with ammunition to a field. When we landed, we noted the troops had funny uniforms and were standing around with their mouths open. They were North Koreans and had just taken the field! They were so surprised, they did not even try to stop us when we took off. Another time, a field had been evacuated, although our Army still controlled the area. A jeep with a radio was left behind to direct the arriving supply planes. When you rolled in, the radio said, "This is Corporal So and So, base commander speaking!"

A couple of things at the time were not so funny, but now after forty years, everything seems less tragic. The Army was in bad shape for mortar shells. The code name for the shells was graham crackers. You guessed it; we arrived with a planeload of graham crackers. The Army was close to stringing us up. I have always liked graham crackers, so I liberated a few boxes.

During some very bad weather, one of our planes was making a GCA approach to Kimpo Air Base. It was low tide and it landed in the bay. No one was hurt and they waded into shore. Japanese guards were put on the plane to guard the mail. They crawled up on the bags inside the plane to sleep, the tide came in, and they all drowned.

Margaret Higgins was a very well-known correspondent at that time. Whatever she wanted to do, she did it. One night, she flew back from Korea with us. Rooms were very scarce, so one of the guys let her have his and he came in with me. Later, she called in her story to New York. After listening to it, I asked her as she passed my room if she wasn't ashamed to call in something so dumb. Her answer was that's what the people want to hear, so that's what I give them. On the same note, one of Bob Hope's starlets got off the plane with us with a bandaged hand. She told everyone she burned her hand washing her mess kit with the boys. Truth was, she was blind drunk and, falling down, she grabbed the chimney of the heating stove. The media played up her little washing story.

Leaflets cut and ready to be bundled or rolled for use in bombs.

National Archives

THE 6167TH OPERATIONS SQUADRON

BILL KLOPP, 6167th Ops Sq, B Flight (The 6167th evolved from the Kyushu Gypsies. They pursued PSY-WAR missions late in the war.)—Some Headquarters types would come from Tokyo on the 30th or 31st of the month and leave the 1st or 2nd to collect two months of combat pay. All you needed was one day in the combat zone to qualify.

I flew PSYWAR missions from K-16 from March to August 1952. Our code name was ANZAC. We hauled leaflets for the 8240th Army Unit in Seoul, who were the Army guys who provided the leaflets, kickers, loudspeaker girls, et cetera. There was a Ranger unit who furnished jump masters, agents, weapons, and explosives in unlimited quantity and variety, with accounting or hand receipts. The 3rd Air Rescue Squadron was across the field in helos and SA-16s. We drove the speaker over the MLR at night, delivered supplies to Cho-do, Peng Yang–do, and Yo-do (islands off the northeast coast of Korea, north of the bomb line, where the USAF had flight recovery sites and small outposts), and inserted folks who wanted to go north and walk home. It was a good outfit, although living conditions were somewhat as depicted by the *M*A*S*H* TV show. As I recall, we lost no aircraft during my time there, although I got a couple of hits, once while delivering the Sunday newspapers to Pyongyang, and we had one C-47 named Patches because it had over 100 of same covering enemy-induced holes in its skin. I got eighty-one missions in only 142 hours, a DFC and AM with three OLC and made IP [instruction pilot] as a twenty-three-year-old second lieutenant, and the assignment of my choice later on.

Our sister unit, A Flight, was the lamplighter flare droppers at K-14. I took a couple of rides with them, but that seemed pretty dull. Most of us went with orders as lamplighters but were siphoned off to PSYWAR at Fuchu. Our gang was rather hush-hush at the time, although there was an article in *Time* about those who flew "unarmed and unafraid in transport aircraft" deep into enemy territory. We were neither, of course, and even developed our own armament: an air-cooled .50-caliber machine gun in the back door and "presentos," which were metal ammunition boxes packed with C-3 and RDX explosives, nuts and bolts, broken glass, et cetera, detonated by a blasting cap and fuse liberated from the leaflet bundles. Made a hell of a bang. When anyone shot at us en route home from the far north, we'd circle about and deliver a presento or two.

We lived in Quonset huts—two oil stoves per hut for the winter. Had outdoor plumbing—outhouses— and communal washing and shower areas. Did have houseboys to make the beds and do the laundry. Lots of sandbags about, but didn't need them by the time I was there. Bedcheck Charlie did come by once in a while and the AA guns around the field would pop at him now and then, but I don't recall ever getting out of bed or going to a revetment when he visited and don't think anyone else did, either. There was more danger and more awakening noise from the spent AA falling than from whatever he dropped. Seoul was sort of beat up at that time and Young Dung Po, the town just out of K-16, was not the garden spot of the world. Booze and other forms of sin occupied most of what little spare time we had. Didn't do much but fly, eat, drink, and sleep—maybe take a plane to Japan for its 100-hour inspection for a few days off. The airplanes, Ops, O Club, mess hall, and latrine were all within seventy to eighty yards of my tent, so life was pretty convenient.

Local men were the leaflet "kickers," some of whom had 400-plus missions while I was there. Leaflets were stacked in bundles—about fifteen by twelve by nine inches—and wrapped with brown kraft paper and tied with twine. In the twine knot was tied a dynamite blasting cap with about one foot of fuse. At the end of the fuse was an igniter; pull the pin and the fuse was lit. We delivered at 6,000 feet up to 8,000 feet AGL and the cap was supposed to blow the bundle open at about 2,000 feet to distribute the paper. We appropriated these same caps and fuses for our presentos but delivered them a great deal lower. Never delivered

presentos or shot at them [the enemy] while on a propaganda mission—bad form; we were friends then.

We could leave after seventy-five missions. I had
allocated most of my pay home and I had to do nine
more missions to pay my mess bill, et cetera. Getting
two or three missions a day was not uncommon. That's
how guys could get their required seventy-five missions and go home in ninety days.

HAROLD GILBERT, 43rd TCS—I was a C-46 pilot
based at Brady Field in Japan. I spent two weeks as an
additional duty with B Flight at K-16. There were
leaflet drops, agent drops, flare drops over the MSR in
support of B-26 bombing missions. We also supported
the Army by dropping flares to illuminate the enemy
during some of their night flights, and we flew supplies
to islands above the "line" that had radar and radio
units. We lost one C-46 early in the program. At either
LITTLE SWITCH or BIG SWITCH, some of the
crew members emerged. Their story confirmed what
we thought might have happened. A double agent had
tossed a grenade into the tail section just as he departed
the airplane. The grenade disabled the flight controls
and the crew had to bail out. They were then captured.

THE PWD AMPHIBIOUS LANDING

By March 1951, UN forces were battering Communist forces,
but at a high cost in lives and equipment. The Psychological
Warfare Division at Eighth Army Headquarters wondered if it
could do something to reduce the opposition. It devised a plan

to get the Communists to move some of their forces from the front line. The Eighth Army would simulate preparations for an amphibious landing on the eastern coast.

Surrender leaflets were dropped in large numbers well behind the current lines but near the beaches where the simulated landing was to take place. The leaflets were the same ones that the United Nations dropped just before a major assault. It was hoped that the enemy would suspect a new front was about to open. The Navy increased its activity in the area, and aircraft sorties began a false target preparation by bombing and softening targets close to the beaches. The campaign was limited by the lack of resources in the PWD, but the goal was partly accomplished in that some enemy troops were moved from the front to cover the beach access.

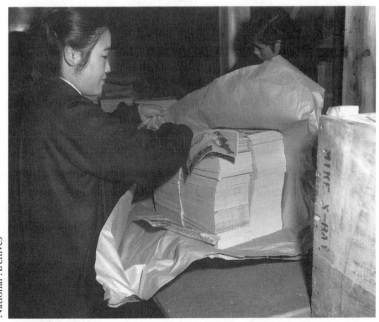

National Archives

A leaflet bundle is prepared at the FEC printing plant in Yokohama, Japan, for a drop over a friendly area.

National Archives

Soldiers of the Printing and Publication Sections roll leaflets, April 1952.

OPERATION MOOLAH

When the Russian MIG-15 jet fighter appeared in the Korean War during November 1950, the entire UN air forces were immediately outclassed.[6] The MIG could fly faster than South Korea's World War II–vintage F-51s, the UN forces' new F-80 Shooting Star, and the Navy's F9F Panther. Even with the newest US fighter, the F-86 Sabre, which was just entering production and in short supply, the UN air forces were still at a disadvantage. In a dogfight, the MIG had a higher initial accel-eration than the Sabre and could outdistance it in a dive, even with the Sabre's higher terminal velocity. The MIG was just as powerful as the F-86 but, being lighter, it was much more maneuverable and it was an excellent daytime air superiority fighter. The Sabre had maneuvering advantage at lower altitudes. UN forces managed to hold the advantage, however, with carefully selected air combat tactics, superior pilots, and, later, modifications to the Sabre.

Early in the war, it was highly possible that the MIGs were flown by Soviets, even though the Soviet Union was officially neutral in the conflict. UN pilots thought they heard Russian being spoken on radio frequencies used by the MIGs and re-turning POWs said they had been interrogated by Soviet pilots. Besides, the MIG was new and the Chinese and North Koreans probably were not yet trained on it.

With its large cannon, the MIG was deadly against a large formation of B-29 bombers, a fact that US military planners and the Strategic Air Command recognized. The MIG-15 and its successors were top-line fighters, typical of those expected to defend the Soviet Union against incoming bombers. US strategic planning against the Soviet Union depended on long-range bomber attacks by B-29s, B-59s, and B-36s, so the capa-bilities of the MIG were of great concern. Since the MIG had never been seen outside of the Soviet Union before, our tech-nical knowledge of it was poor, but an understanding of its per-formance expectations and design philosophies was necessary in order to formulate appropriate tactics and defensive systems. The Chinese never flew over UN lines, so there was no wreck-age to be found and studied. We needed to have one in our hands so that we could fly it, take it apart, and get to know the minds that designed it. (Two MIGs were flown to Denmark by Polish pilots, but those were noncombat training versions and were returned immediately without having been flown.)

The first chance to see a MIG up close, other than in a

Sabre's gun sight, was after one crashed on a sandbar. The pilot ejected, but the fighter maintained a shallow descent and eventually ditched into the sea, coming to rest on a large sandbar. Exposed at low tide, it was largely intact, though not flyable, and the UN command formed OPERATION MIG to recover the wreckage before the sea dragged it away or the North Koreans destroyed it.

British navy ships, including the carrier *Eagle* and the cruiser *Birmingham*, assisted by small craft from the South Korean navy and a special barge from Japan, retrieved the MIG. It was taken to Pusan Airfield, dismantled, and taken to Wright Patterson Air Force Base in Ohio for testing. It provided volumes of information about Russian jet fighter design and manufacture, but it could have provided more valuable information if it had still been able to fly. We needed to get our hands on a flyable MIG.

What some term the greatest PSYWAR triumph in the Korean War was hatched (according to General Mark Clark) in the correspondent's billet in early 1952 by a war correspondent musing the problem over a bottle of brandy. Historically, the Chinese soldier had always been susceptible to *silver bullets*, or bribes. Why not bribe one of their pilots to bring a MIG to us? His idea was written up as a fictional interview with an Air Force general, intended as a satirical joke.

Later that year, the interview was sent to the Headquarters of the Far East Air Forces in Japan, which thought it was a credible idea and forwarded the plan to Washington. It made the rounds of the Pentagon and the State Department and was approved by the Joint Chiefs of Staff on 20 March 1953. The plan was staffed and approved by the Joint Psychological Committee at Far East Command in Tokyo and forwarded to the commanding general of UN forces in Korea, General Clark. He had heard of the idea in an Army memo dated November 1952 and was already planning for it. He approved the plan and titled it OPERATION MOOLAH.

Rolled leaflets are loaded into bombs, April 1952.

National Archives

Private Mason, X Corps, shows how a roll of PSYWAR leaflets is carried in
105mm artillery shells, Tokyo, November 1950.

The plan was to offer $50,000 to any pilot who flew a
combat-capable MIG to South Korea. The first pilot to do so
would receive an additional $50,000. Of course, the pilot
would be granted complete political asylum. Such a defection

would be an enormous propaganda windfall. The pilot would be characterized as fleeing the authoritarian society of North Korea to the freedom of the South. It would play on North Korean and Chinese paranoia and cause them to mistrust and possibly ground some of their pilots.

The Soviet Union claimed that none of its pilots was flying against the United Nations, but UN pilots had heard Russian over their radios during dogfights with MIGs. The UN command was certain Soviets were flying against UN fighters and it suspected that many were top-notch pilots, or Honchos, as our pilots called them. If we could get one to fly his jet to Kimpo airfield, what a propaganda victory that would be!

OPERATION MOOLAH was announced by General Clark over UN radio in April 1953. The shortwave broadcast was repeated in Russian, Chinese, and Korean to contact any possible MIG pilot. The timing was deliberate. The armistice talks had just restarted and there had just been a large exchange of sick and wounded POWs in OPERATION LITTLE SWITCH. The talks were going poorly. The North Koreans were tough and inflexible, and they were adept at playing psychological games to vex the UN team. Things were going nowhere. A defecting MIG pilot would cause a serious loss of face for the North Koreans and give the UN side an advantage when it was needed most.

On 23 and 26 April, more than a million leaflets were dropped on airfields in the Yalu River basin. A half-million leaflets were deposited on the Sinuiju and Uiju airfields on 10 and 18 May. These leaflets offered:

. . . the sum of 50,000 U.S. dollars to any pilot who delivers a modern, operational, combat-type jet aircraft in flyable condition to South Korea. The first pilot who delivers such a jet aircraft to the free world will receive an additional 50,000 U.S. dollars bonus for his bravery.

Additional notations in Chinese and Korean said:

This is a message from the Americans to any jet pilot who can read Russian. If you know such a person, please give it to him. It tells him how to escape to the UN forces.[7]

We especially wanted a Soviet pilot.

Shortly after OPERATION MOOLAH started, the Russian-language broadcasts were blocked by a powerful jammer in North Korea. Oddly, the Chinese- and Korean-language transmissions were not jammed. MIG flights dropped drastically. For eight days, there were no MIG sorties at all, an unprecedented stand down. The flying weather was terrible from 28 April to 7 May, but the stand down was probably at least partially due to OPERATION MOOLAH. A large formation of MIGs was sighted on 30 April, more than 160 planes, but they were reluctant to fight and three were shot down by UN Sabres. Perhaps they were being flown by new Korean and Chinese pilots being checked on an emergency basis. Before the broadcasts, MIGs encountered over Korea were generally painted with the solid red star of the Soviet air force, but after the offer, only North Korean or Chinese markings were noted. Perhaps the Soviet pilots were withdrawn from the Korean front, their superiors fearing the consequences of a defection. Finally, Kim Il Sung, the North Korean leader, triumphantly said in a radio speech that brave North Korean pilots were assuming a larger role in the air battle.

There were far fewer missions in the ninety days following OPERATION MOOLAH than in the ninety days preceding it, and the quality of the MIG pilots was noticeably poorer after regular sorties resumed in mid-May. It was obvious that the excellent Soviet pilots were no longer flying. After OPERATION MOOLAH, the MIG pilots compiled the worst record of the entire war. UN Sabres downed 165 MIGs to only three losses, a fifty-five-to-one ratio! Perhaps the Koreans were only letting the most politically trustworthy pilots fly, which may have kept their best pilots on the ground. But no MIG pilot defected.

The armistice was signed and OPERATION MOOLAH was forgotten. The results had been positive, though no MIG was recovered. Two months later, on 23 September 1953 at 0924 hours, Captain Ro Kum Suk of the North Korean Air Force flew his MIG low to avoid radar detection, landed at Kimpo airfield, and asked for political asylum. The fighter was a MIG-15bis, a later production model that had been superseded by the MIG-17. Captain Ro had never heard of the $50,000 offer. He was motivated by hatred for his Soviet and Chinese "advisers."

The United Nations was embarrassed by the defection, due to the delicate nature of the armistice, and immediately withdrew its offer, but it fully exploited the psychological value of the event. It offered to return the MIG to "its rightful owner." The North Koreans were trying to get the Soviet Union recognized as a neutral party at the armistice talks to speak on their behalf, so the North Koreans could not acknowledge ownership of Soviet-built planes. They wanted to claim that the Soviet Union had never been involved in the war; the MIG was solid proof that it had. Captain Ro's MIG is now on display in the Air Force Museum in Dayton, Ohio.

President Eisenhower was not in favor of OPERATION MOOLAH. He thought it was unethical to offer money to a defector; he should defect for ideological reasons.[8] General Clark wrote in his Korean memoirs that he believed it was ethical because it was made in the open and the reward was paid as promised. Soviet propaganda declared it was a cheap trick and against international law, sure signs of their irritation over the event. To the Koreans, it was business as usual. Chinese and Korean warlords were known to buy off opposing troops and the notion of the fee was long established in Korean and Chinese commerce. To satisfy Eisenhower, the CIA devised a plan

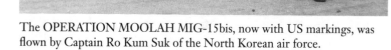

The OPERATION MOOLAH MIG-15bis, now with US markings, was flown by Captain Ro Kum Suk of the North Korean air force.

whereby Captain Ro would openly reject the reward money in exchange for quietly receiving technical education benefits and other financial considerations equal to the reward.

Captain Ro provided many details about NKAF movements that were vital negotiating levers in the armistice talks. The North Koreans had been transferring fighters from Manchuria to North Korea in violation of the armistice agreements. The North Koreans claimed the transfers were allowed because the airfields were civilian. The planes went back to Manchuria.

Captain Ro later received a job with a CIA front organization called the Committee for Free Asia.

OPERATION MOOLAH was hailed as the greatest PSYWAR operation of the war, even though the pilot didn't defect directly as a result of it and then only after the war was in recess. Though some declared MOOLAH an unethical stunt, it served to destroy the international reputation of the Soviet

Union as a peaceful bystander. The MIG was proof that the Soviets actively supported North Korea, which everyone had known but could not prove. Combined with the fact that hundreds of North Korean POWs refused to go back to North Korea after the armistice, Captain Ro's defection was proof to the world that North Korea was not the paradise that Communist propaganda claimed it to be.

The scientific and technical intelligence value of the MIG was huge, despite the fact that it no longer was the latest variant.[9] Since the armistice was fragile, it could fall apart at any time and then Sabres would face MIGs again. The Americans had to find out how the airplane flew. The MIG was taken in secret to Kadena Air Force Base on Okinawa where two US test pilots flew the fighter to find out what it could do. (One was Chuck Yeager, who later became the first man to break the sound barrier.) With a little instruction from Captain Ro, they flew the MIG against current US jet fighters.

Most of the flights were white knuckle because the weather was terrible and Soviet engineering shaky: a narrow flight window, touchy engine controls, unreliable instruments. In the course of the test flights, several myths about the aircraft were blown. It could not go supersonic, it had a terrible roll rate, control was marginal at high speeds and high altitudes, and the canopy frosted over, severely restricting vision because the hot-air system did not work well. True, the fighter had a high rate of climb and excellent acceleration. It was more maneuverable than the Sabre at slow speeds, could outturn it, and had excellent rough-field landing characteristics, a logistical plus.

All in all, however, the F-86 Sabre was a better fighter. Unfortunately, we didn't have enough F-86s early in the war. Due to the superior pilots, more powerful guns, and sharper tactics, F-86s outgunned the MIGs by more than ten to one. This overwhelming kill ratio caused a serious psychological loss of face for the Chinese. Their soldiers were totally open to attack from the sky, day or night, because the Communists

"Who will take care of you?" asks this UN leaflet.

moved their fighters to sanctuary across the Yalu and this left no fighter cover. A special leaflet was drawn up and dropped on the Chinese and NKPA solders asking them, "Where is your air force?" The MIG retreat meant that the MIG myth was broken. It's better to work with knowledge than guesswork. US fighter tactics were revised to take advantage of the new facts learned about the MIG.

WHY DO THEY SURRENDER?

Korean War–era politicians would have preferred to hear that Communist soldiers surrendered because they had experienced a political conversion, but most did so because food was scarce, equipment was barely adequate, shelter and medical care were practically nonexistent, and because soldiers pressed into service with little training were lonely and didn't know what they were fighting for. Soldiers ate cotton from their first aid kits to stop their stomachs from rumbling. Conditions got so bad for the Communist soldier that he was willing to risk death for the paper promise of food and humane treatment. Political reasons were scarce. United Nations PSYWAR leaflets and other propaganda played on the soldiers' needs, and they promised that, by surrendering, soldiers would see their families after the war. The signature of the commanding general on the pass was assurance that it was genuine.

One of the most famous Korean War leaflets was the "safe conduct pass," often printed with one side resembling paper money to ensure that it would be picked up. These were dropped over masses of North Korean and Chinese troops, and they stressed that the soldiers would be treated humanely if they crossed the lines carrying one of the passes. Thousands did, even though they were threatened with execution by their officers if they picked one up.

The text of the pass was in Korean, Chinese, and English:

Attention all soldiers of the United Nations Forces. This leaflet guarantees humane treatment to any North Korean desiring to cease fighting. Take this man to your nearest commissioned officer at once.[10]

A Communist soldier usually picked up a safe conduct pass weeks before he used it and hid it in his uniform. The pass never expired. By the time he surrendered, he was so fed up with his conditions that he had no fear of the enemy. Political officers tried to ensure that they would not lose their soldiers to surrender. Before a battle, rations were increased and political indoctrination intensified, an attempt at control through the mind and the belly. They told their men that UN soldiers would torture and kill them on sight. It was also suggested that a soldier's family would suffer if he surrendered. The NKPA soldier fought because he thought he had no other choice. The safe conduct pass gave him a choice. Sometimes, the same officer who had threatened them weeks before led a group to UN positions in a mass surrender.[11]

TOM DREW, D-2-7, 1st Marine Div—I was a buck sergeant on the western front during the "stalemate" of 1952. We dug in on "Jamestown" and had outposts in No Man's Land to occupy, plus a listening post. Occasionally we went looking for trouble with a reinforced company. Sometimes on patrol into No Man's Land, we would, in essence, flood the area with surrender leaflets. I didn't particularly care for this, as it let the enemy know where we were, therefore [inviting] an ambush the next night.

To counter leaflets showing POWs receiving medical aid, Communist political officers explained that the men shown

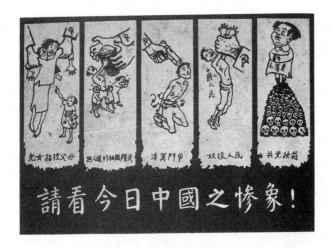

Two complicated UN leaflets tell the Chinese soldier that he is the tool of outside forces. The top leaflet reminds him he was taken from his family, the Communist government takes his family's food, he may be shot by his officers, and he is totally in the control of the Communists. The last panel says Mao Tse-tung is building his empire on the bodies of men just like him. The lower cartoon repeats the common theme: The Soviet Union gives arms to China, which forces the common man to fight in a war. He works hard but just gets shot at. Finally, a happier Chinese soldier crosses to the UN side holding a safe conduct pass.

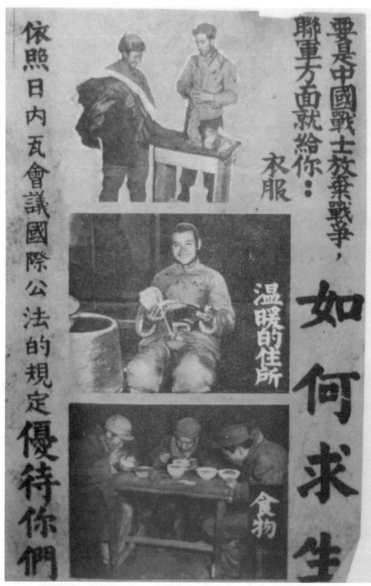

要是中國戰士放棄戰爭，
聯軍方面就給你：衣服
溫暖的住所
食物
如何求生
依照日內瓦會議國際公法的規定優待你們

The UN used this leaflet to promise warm clothing, comfortable conditions, and good food to any surrendering Chinese soldier.

were actually being injected with germs in hideous experiments. Soldiers were told the leaflets were intentionally saturated with disease organisms so that they wouldn't be picked up for toilet paper, cigarette wrappers, or starting fires.

Early in the war, illustrated UN leaflets had black bars across the faces of POWs to hide their identity and thereby avoid reprisals in the camps. The United Nations soon learned that Communist political officers were explaining that the black bars were there to hide the scars from disfiguring chemical warfare experiments, so, with the permission of the pictured POW, the bars were removed.

Translation by Steven Rook

1. This is from the UN, to you soldiers. If you have a friend you can trust, please let him read it, too. 2. If you want to escape, try it at night. 3. The UN soldiers will warmly welcome you. 4. Please come safely and the UN will give you food, a warm place, and medical treatment. You will be happy and welcome.

WALTER MORRISON, 24th Div MP—My duty was to screen refugees going from North Korea to South Korea, and to sort out NKPA and CCF soldiers from the civilians. I was shown hundreds of safe conduct passes and surrender leaflets we had dropped on North Korea. The Chinese soldiers were shot by their officers if they were found with one of these leaflets on them. They sewed them into their uniforms and put them up their rectums to escape detection.

OPERATION FARMER

OPERATION FARMER was a PSYWAR effort aimed at North Korean farmers, who reportedly were upset with the high taxes and crop share that they were forced to pay to their government. South Korea was the breadbasket of the peninsula, and without access to those crops, North Korea had to feed itself with the relatively poor farms in the north. The leaflets encouraged farmers to hide parts of their crops so their families could eat better. They also suggested that farmers should sell some of their harvest on the black market. The OPERATION tilted the already fragile North Korean agricultural economy even further toward failure.

B-29S, PLAN STRIKE, AND PLAN BLAST

B-29s often dropped leaflet bombs during normal bombing missions, especially those against factories and major military supply depots. In a sixteen-plane mission, one plane would carry leaflets. In later operations, when the B-29s had more varied duties such as bombing by the Shoran radio guidance unit and testing airborne radar, several sorties were always reserved for leaflet drops, or "paper routes."

During the summer of 1951, under orders from the Joint Chiefs of Staff, leaflets warning civilians to evacuate were dropped on Pyongyang, Chinnampo, Wonsan, and Kanggye before major bomber strikes against fuel and ammo depots and railway yards. This was a PLAN BLAST mission, an attempt to reduce civilian casualties. It was also intended to lower civilian morale and disrupt industrial production. In addition, the fleeing civilians would clog roads and delay the North Korean army.

Two bombing/PSYWAR operations were planned. PLAN STRIKE was the name given to the attacks against communication centers and main supply routes and their warning leaflet operation. PLAN BLAST was the attacks against Pyongyang and its military targets along with its warning leaflet operation. The same tactic had been used successfully by General Curtis LeMay before bomber raids in Germany in the last days of World War II. If a leaflet drop was part of the mission, it would precede the bombers by one to three days to warn those in the target area, "Look out! Here it comes! Better leave." After the mission, another B-29 mission would drop leaflets that said, "Told you so!"

Some politicians and military planners in Washington thought that the leaflet campaign was not enough to guarantee that the civilians would be warned. Before one of the PLAN STRIKE missions, Radio Seoul also warned residents of two towns on the target list, Sinchon and Yonan, of the upcoming B-29 mission. Later, General Glenn Barcus of Bomber Command also released the names of seventy-eight additional targeted cities to the radio and the press. The intent was humanitarian, but many authorities were alarmed. The State Department was worried that the Communists would make their own propaganda use of the warning. The mass attacks against towns with military targets could be turned around to look like attacks against civilians, warned or not. The world press stressed the inhumanity of bombing urban areas and failed to see the humane intent of the leaflet missions that were meant to allow the populace to escape the bombing of an urban target. Future announcements concentrated on the military nature of targets and no further notice of any mass attack was made. Occasionally, civilians were still warned by leaflet drops.

The leaflet missions often were used after major operations to capitalize on the trauma caused by the attack. After the Inchon landing, for example, thirteen B-29s were assigned to drop surrender leaflets on the retreating North Koreans and more than 100 soldiers surrendered in one group, all carrying B-29 safe conduct passes.[12]

R.W. KOCH, 581st ARC—[Under the command of Colonel John K. Arnold, Jr.,] the 581st dropped lots of leaflets plus Oriental agents into many areas of the Far East until Colonel Arnold was shot down in his B-29 and compromised the 581st in a coerced confession. Their black B-29s and SA-16s operated out of Clark Field, PI; Kadena, Okinawa; and Yakota, Japan. They cooperated with the CIA until that agency secured its own aircraft. The files on Colonel Arnold are currently being reviewed for declassification and public release by the USAF Historical Research Center.

PLANS STRIKE and BLAST were not universally accepted by Far East Air Force (FEAF) commanders. Some thought they lost the element of surprise with the leaflets and that placed their B-29s and B-26s in greater danger from ground defenses. It was also true that the North Koreans prevented the populace from escaping, so their protection was never fully realized, but the disruption of industrial production was achieved. In small numbers, people still left the factories and escaped to villages.

The Communists did use the attacks to their advantage. Radio Peking denounced the raids as a blanket bombing

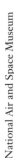

Mechanics load an M16-A1 leaflet bomb into the bay of a B-26.

against civilians under the pretense of military targeting. *Pravda*, the Communist Party newspaper in the Soviet Union, released several editorials to the world Communist press calling the raids unethical pressure on the truce negotiations. The Communists were worried about civilian morale and the bombing had made it worse. *Pravda* said the factories were the only way North Korea could progress beyond its agricultural past and the United Nations was actually trying to deprive the country of its chance to move into the modern world. There were even more charges of genocide.

Actually, the attacks were very effective PSYWAR. They demonstrated that UN forces had control of the skies and could attack any target they chose, and that the North Koreans were powerless to stop them. Some people reportedly abandoned their factory jobs and slipped back to safer lives in the country.

There also were several B-29 incendiary raids on Pyongyang on 5 and 6 January 1951. A snowfall slowed the firestorm,
but more than 35 percent of the city center was burned. Pyongyang radio reported, however, that the fire burned for two days,
causing severe loss of civilian life, a claim unsubstantiated by
UN intelligence.[13]

The United Nations countered with claims that its leaflet
drops proved that the missions were purely military. However,
it was almost impossible to overcome the claims of the Communists, especially when they were supported by newsreels
showing blown-up houses, schools, and hospitals as well as
dead and wounded children. It was no matter that the newsreels may not have been filmed after the actual raid in question;
the argument was almost impossible to win.

Bomber Command's last missions over North Korea on
27 July 1953 were leaflet flights. Before the cease-fire at 2201
hours, two RB-29s from the 98th Wing and two from the 91st
Wing dropped leaflets in a "paper route" over North Korea.
The last flight was commanded by Lieutenant Denver Cook. A
leaflet drop had been one of the first UN aircraft missions of
the war and now it was also the last.

THE CHINESE CASUALTY LEAFLET

One of the "weapons" in the Chinese arsenal was a tactic called
"human sea waves" used to terrorize opposing forces. They
would pour hundreds of troops ahead in a battle, even in the
face of terrible UN firepower. Some troops in the following
waves were unarmed and expected to find rifles as they advanced among their dead comrades. The loss of life was stag-
gering. General Ridgway was disturbed by this huge waste of
human life, even though the dead were enemy soldiers. He ordered a psychological attack be made on enemy soldiers with
leaflets showing their masses of dead. The intent was to destroy
their willingness to make further hopeless charges.

He suggested that the leaflets carry gruesome pictures of

"Count your dead!" suggests this UN leaflet to the Communists.

dead Chinese soldiers to emphasize the futility of headlong mass attacks. Opinion in the Psychological Warfare Branch was mixed. Some thought the general should get what he ordered. Others thought the pictures might evoke the wrong response—a hatred of Americans and a desire for revenge. Atrocity propaganda could beget atrocities. The PWB decided to try to design a leaflet to meet General Ridgway's request.

One of the problems was the selection of the photograph. Most US Army photos showed US soldiers standing next to the heaps of Chinese dead after a wave attack. They were taken for publicity purposes and often the soldiers were smiling—not what was needed for the leaflet. A photo was finally found that simply showed the Chinese dead as they had fallen. The photo clearly showed the Chinese uniforms, many stained with blood. The caption on the back of the picture sealed the decision. It read: "Battlefield scene, showing Chinese Communist dead on Korean Hill 262, after successful assault by Turkish RCT [Regimental Combat Team], February 21, 1951."[14]

Few Communist soldiers seemed to realize that they were facing anyone other than US or South Korean troops. Actually, there were troops from twelve UN countries, all in combat positions. The photo not only would prove to the Chinese that they faced certain death from fearsome UN weaponry; it would prove that nations other than the United States and South Korea were allied against them.

The text was drafted and translated into Chinese. A short message was placed alongside the photo. It said, "These Chinese needlessly met death resisting UN Turkish forces." A longer message was on the back. Thousands of copies were dropped over Chinese lines.

Later, a group was assembled from recently captured Chinese soldiers to assess the impact of the UN leaflet operations, including the Chinese casualty leaflet. The POWs were first asked to discuss the effect of each leaflet's text and how easily it could be read and understood. Next, they were asked about the effectiveness of the photo or diagram in conveying the leaflet's theme, especially among illiterate POWs. Last, interrogators sought the overall effect of the leaflet on Chinese fighting efficiency and will.

All the POWs agreed that the text of the casualty leaflet was easily read and understood. The message that they would die if they continued to fight was clear, and the picture depicted a scene that was common to the battlefield and understood by Chinese soldiers. They agreed that the leaflet was powerful. But the POWs didn't believe the picture; they were sure it was a lie. They were certain there were no more Turkish troops in Korea because the Chinese had killed all of them in their initial incursion across the Yalu River in November 1951.

On 25 and 26 November 1951, Chinese forces did attack the Turkish RCT north of Pyongyang, killing many but not all. Most were scattered by the force of the attack, but the RCT was reconstituted after several weeks. Initial press reports said the Turks had been wiped out, and the Chinese political officers had used these press releases in their indoctrination to the troops. Because the Chinese POWs were convinced that the Turks had all been killed, the leaflet, which they initially thought was powerful, fell apart, though it carried nothing but the truth. The leaflet is a classic example of why PSYWAR messages need to be tested on a sample population before they are distributed.

It's interesting that the same picture was used again in another leaflet, with an edited caption. This time it said: "The fire-sea will crush your human-sea tactics." The text on the back continued: "Your life is your most treasured possession. Why lose your life in battle? Your attack has long been expected. True, you are advancing now, but look around you at your hundreds of dead comrades. They will not enjoy life again! The UN's "Fire Sea" will again crush the flesh and blood of your human wave tactics. Will you be alive to see the sun rise tomorrow? It is better to surrender now and live!"[15]

There was no mention of Turks or any nationality this time.

MOSQUITOES

The Fifth Air Force and the Navy used World War II–vintage propeller aircraft, including the F-51 Mustang and the Corsair. The T-6 Texan was a training aircraft, not a fighter, but it played a large tactical PSYWAR role. During the Korean War, T-6s were forward observer aircraft, finding targets for the fighters and bombers and guiding them in. In Korea, they were nicknamed the Mosquito Squadron. The pilots often rolled their canopies back and tossed leaflets to enemy troops.

After the Inchon landing, when the North Koreans were rapidly being driven back north, one Mosquito pilot managed to persuade nearly 200 North Koreans to surrender with only one piece of paper. Lieutenant George Nelson spotted them near Kunsan and swooped low over their heads. They didn't look too belligerent and he had an idea. He hurriedly wrote a note telling them to drop their guns and move to a nearby hill. He signed the note "MacArthur." To his surprise, they complied! He found a UN patrol in the area and directed it to the waiting North Koreans. No doubt the soldiers were weary of the pounding they were taking after Inchon and were eager to surrender.

SPECIAL OPERATIONS RESEARCH OFFICE

After the armistice, the Army ran many studies of the effectiveness and performance of its forces and operations, including PSYWAR. One study conducted by Carl Berger, *An Introduction to Wartime Leaflets*, was published in 1959. It included leaflet operations in the world wars and Korea and drew several conclusions, some not too surprising. It reported that leaflets were valid aids to wartime objectives if integrated with other military operations. PSYWAR planners needed access to intelligence, and the operations required the backing of all levels of command. Friendly troops needed to understand the PSYWAR campaign and be instructed to follow the promises made in the leaflets.

National Air and Space Museum

Leaflets stream from a Kyushu Gypsy C-47, possibly over the Yalu River on the Chinese border, November 1950.

Berger points out several other findings from his study concerning the message, dissemination methods, and the need for further research. The content of the message is of utmost importance and must be tested against a sample of the target audience. It should be interesting, true, and credible. It should not ridicule the enemy but rather praise him for his bravery in order to win his trust. Simple messages are best, with pictures included for illiterate or semiliterate audiences; long political essays are ineffective. Predictions about future events are risky because credibility is lost if the prediction doesn't come true. Whatever the message, it may be used by the enemy to his advantage.

In order to have successful PSYWAR dissemination during a crisis, the Army needs to develop and practice methods during peacetime that make use of the most up-to-date aircraft and artillery. Pilots, who sometimes dislike leaflet missions, should be properly indoctrinated and trained ahead of time, and air units should be devoted to leaflet operations for greatest effectiveness.

Research between conflicts on cultural symbols and communication patterns in possible conflict areas will ensure successful leaflet operations during a war.

1. Carl Berger's *An Introduction to Wartime Leaflets* details the history of leaflets in full, from the American Revolution to the days after the Korean War. No other book gives as much organized detail on leaflets.

2. These numbers are from Berger, *Wartime Leaflets*, though several other sources present identical numbers, which may mean that they are originally from a US government press release.

3. Sections 2 through 5 of Berger's *Wartime Leaflets* discuss leaflet types and give many examples of each, including those not used during the Korean War.

4. Berger presents an interesting comparison between news leaflets used in Korea and those from other eras. There were strenuous efforts in South Korea to report the news faithfully. These "newspapers" were often the only source of news for frontline troops from both sides and for civilians.

5. Translated by Steven Rook from a Korean War leaflet. The text is typical of the surrender appeal. It usually underscored the mortal dangers of war and suggested that the smart thing for the soldier to do was to extract himself from the war by surrendering.

6. Berger briefly discusses the OPERATION MOOLAH leaflet in *Wartime Leaflets*. The best sources, however, are General Mark Clark's memoir, *From the Danube to the Yalu* (New York: Harper & Bros., 1954, 1988); Callum A. MacDonald's *Korea: The War before*

Vietnam (New York: The Free Press/Macmillan, 1986); and Robert Frank Futrell's indispensable history of the air war in Korea, *The United States Air Force in Korea 1950–1953* (New York: Duell, Sloan and Pearce, 1961). General Clark's book is perhaps the most revealing, since his Headquarters originated and carried out the operation.

7. The text of the MOOLAH leaflet was in several languages so that it could be read by anyone who picked it up. Leaflets often carried English translations to assure that US troops would understand the promises made in them.

8. See General Mark Clark, *From the Danube to the Yalu.*

9. See an initial report on the MIG in Appendix 1. General Chuck Yeager and Leo Janos include a brief story on the test flights in *Yeager, an Autobiography* (New York: Bantam Books, 1985).

10. Translation by Steven Rook of a safe conduct pass.

11. "Psychological Warfare in Korea," pp. 65–75.

12. Wallace Brown's *The Endless Hours: My Two and a Half Years as a Prisoner of the Chinese Communists* (New York: Norton, 1961) is a moving account of a STRIKE B-29 that was shot down during one of these missions. It describes the capture and imprisonment of the crew members and their eventual repatriation.

13. Futrell, *US Air Force in Korea*, p. 258.

14. Translated in PWS leaflet summaries.

15. Translated in PWS leaflet summaries.

4

Radio and the News

The propaganda radio station was the second most active UN PSYWAR activity during the Korean War. First established in Japan soon after the NKPA crossed the 38th parallel, radio operations involved studio and mobile productions in several dialects of Korean, Chinese, and Russian.

VOICE OF THE UN COMMAND (VUNC)

The Voice of the UN Command, or VUNC, went on the air at 1240, 1270, 2635, and 3985 kilohertz from a studio in Tokyo on 29 June 1950, four days after the North Koreans invaded the South.[1]

The operation was created from available resources by the seven-man Special Projects Branch, Far East Command, G2, headed by Colonel Woodall Greene. (This organization was later named the Psychological Warfare Branch.) On the morning of 29 June, the FEC psychological warfare officer, Major Thomas Mathews, was told by Colonel Greene to prepare thirty minutes of PSYWAR radio material for broadcast to Korea that night. Borrowing transmitters, finding translators, and ripping news copy from Teletypes, they went on the air eleven hours later, at 2100 hours, broadcasting to the estimated 100,000 radios in Korea.

The studio was borrowed from the Armed Forces Radio Service in Japan and the transmitters were leased from the Broadcasting Corporation of Japan. The translators were found at the Korean Embassy, the Tokyo branch of the Bank of Korea, and the Allied Translator and Interpreter Service. In the chaotic days after the invasion, Korean staff members were hard to find, but Major Mathews located many who had evacuated the Korean Broadcasting System (KBS) in Seoul and fled to Japan.

The initial mission of the station was to reassure South Koreans that help was coming, to call upon North Korea to remove its troops, and to keep all Korean-speaking people informed of the UN position. The studio facilities remained in Tokyo throughout the war, with transmitters in Osaka, Hiroshima, Niigata, Matsue, Fukuoka, and Kagashime. VUNC broadcasts were beamed from the transmitters and relayed from KBS facilities.

One of the initial responsibilities of VUNC was the restoration of the KBS system and its facilities. When work was begun in Pusan to reestablish the KBS, the PWB sent a team of specialists to assist. The Pusan station, HLKB, relayed VUNC and Voice of America broadcasts to the KBS system. After Seoul was retaken in September 1950, VUNC again sent a team to reestablish the KBS facilities. The KBS went back on the air on 1 October 1950, broadcasting from improvised studios in the Bando Hotel. Within a month, it was broadcasting eight hours a day.

Fixed transmitters were highly valued because they were so much more powerful than mobile units. When Radio Pyongyang in North Korea fell to the US 1st Cavalry Division on 22 October 1950, VUNC rapidly dispatched a team to assess the facilities. Radio Pyongyang was fairly up-to-date and was housed in a bunker, so everything was in excellent condition, but finding sufficient coal to run the power plant was a problem. The station was back on the air under UN auspices by 14

National Archives

The latest news is sent via Teletype to Radio Seoul from the 1st RB&L studios, April 1952.

November. Radio Pyongyang broadcast six hours a day until the city fell to the Chinese on 2 December.

As UN forces retreated, UN station personnel salvaged as much equipment as they could, including one of Radio Pyongyang's transmitters. Major Mathews personally destroyed the other transmitter by emptying his pistol several times into it before pulling out. Many North Korean radio personnel chose to defect at this time and fled to the South with the evacuating UN personnel.

A station in Hamhung, North Korea, was well located to transmit to North Korean radios, and the station was in operable condition but lacked a receiver to relay programs from VUNC in Tokyo or the KBS. A receiver was ordered, but fortunately one was quickly found in Hamhung. On 6 December 1950, as a staff was being assembled and the receiver was being installed, electricity in the city was cut off; the Chinese had taken the power station. Power might have been available to the station from a Navy ship in the harbor, but the civilian power grid was also dead, so no one could listen at home. The station was closed down and the staff was evacuated with X Corps from Hamhung Harbor on Christmas Eve 1950. On 4 January Radio Seoul fell as the Communist Chinese forces continued southward.

In late January when the Eighth Army established its own Psychological Warfare Division (PWD), to which was attached the 1st Loudspeaker and Leaflet Company, the PWD assumed the tactical PSYWAR responsibility from the Psychological Warfare Branch (PWB) in Tokyo. By the summer, the PWB had grown to more than fifty-five people and so was renamed the Psychological Warfare Section (PWS), and placed under the assistant chief of staff for operations, the G3. Personnel were always a problem for the PWB/PWS. Translators were found locally, but military personnel were invariably on loan from other organizations and their tenure in the unit was never guaranteed.

In August 1951, the 1st Radio Broadcasting and Leaflet Group—composed of its Headquarters, the 3rd Reproduction Company, and the 4th Mobile Radio Broadcasting Company—attached to the PWS after training at Fort Riley, Kansas, arrived in Korea. The PWS continued overall management of PSYWAR activities in Korea and the 4th took over direct radio operations, with coordination by the Radio Division in the 1st RB&L Headquarters.

A segment of the 1st RB&L was dispatched to Korea in September 1951 as the 8239th Army Unit. Part of its mission

National Archives

At the Radio Tokyo building, the 1st RB&L is on the air with a news program in Chinese. The program director, assistant producer, and special effects director are at the controls, April 1952.

was the refurbishment of Korean radio facilities, which were left in sad shape as UN and CCF forces traded positions. The facilities at Taejon, Taegu, and Pusan were repaired and expanded, and new Japanese transmitters were installed. In Seoul, loudspeakers were placed on poles because of the lack of radios in that war-torn city.

In November, "placation" broadcasting teams were sent to Namwon and the Chiri-san Mountains to help suppress Communist guerrillas. Included were several VUNC aircraft to broadcast appeals to the guerrillas and to drop leaflets to the local people asking them to resist those forces. The bandits relied on the willing and unwilling help of the local populace for food, information, and shelter. If the placation teams could deny them that support, the guerrillas could be stopped.

The teams were particularly successful after a bizarre series of events. They dropped a leaflet to the guerrilla leader Lee Hyun Sang, saying he must give up now because the offer was limited. He didn't give up and was soon killed by the ROK army. Another leaflet was dropped showing a photo of the bullet-riddled Lee Hyun Sang. "Give up or suffer the same fate," the leaflet promised. It was more successful, and many guerrillas surrendered.

Korea is mountainous and radio reception is often poor, so VUNC established a network of low-power transmitters to improve reception in all areas. The equipment included portable five-watt transmitters that followed the tactical battle line. These small installations were vulnerable to enemy action and were moved often. As the network was developed, two transmitter systems emerged. Chinese and North Korean areas were covered by nineteen transmitters in Japan, while twelve South Korean transmitters covered that area.

At this time, daily programming included ninety minutes of news and commentary in Korean and Chinese. The programs were rebroadcast once, for a total of three hours of programming each day. There also was at least one drama each

Margaret An, Yang Hong, Jin Wii, and Tuk Yen broadcast the news in
Chinese from the 1st RB&L Tokyo studios, April 1952.

week. Preparation of the programming was arduous because it
was first assembled and written in English and then translated.
It took about forty-eight man-hours to prepare the daily
ninety-minute program.

After the CCF invasion in November 1951, VUNC began
broadcasting in the Cantonese and Mandarin dialects. Early
after the invasion, VUNC oddly made little reference to the
Chinese directly, preferring the term "a new and fresh army."
Radio Peking had already announced that there were Chinese
"volunteers" in Korea on 4 November. Why VUNC didn't

openly refer to the Chinese is unknown. By 7 November, VUNC began to use "alien Communist" when referring to the Chinese. For example, one news statement read: "The United States charged yesterday that alien Communists have reck-lessly thrown thousands of troops into the war in North Korea." It was not until 12 November that VUNC finally re-ferred to the invaders as Chinese: "The government of Com-munist China has rejected the invitation to be present at the forthcoming debate by the United Nations Security Council on the presence of Communist troops in Korea."

This delay by VUNC points out the relative lack of coor-dination between VUNC, Voice of America, and the Japanese news system. Ten days elapsed between the initial reports of the Chinese on VOA and BCJ before VUNC caught up. VUNC had good coordination with its own elements—the 1st Radio Broadcasting and Leaflet Company, the KBS, and the 8239th Army Unit—but poor operating relationships with agencies outside the Army, and this created friction between VUNC and the external radio systems. The Korean unit of VOA was in New York, which was part of the problem. This friction hurt the effectiveness of the propaganda. People re-ceiving mixed messages become confused and the senders' credibility suffers, an unforgivable PSYWAR sin.

In July 1953, when the South Korean government re-turned to Seoul, VUNC placed its own transmitter there. The 8239th Army Unit consolidated its printing and broadcasting activities at Taekwang High School. VUNC based its mobile radio equipment at Taepyung Ho near the KBS studios, where it remained until 1956. VUNC's mission in Korea expanded with additional transmitters after the armistice. It was dis-banded on 30 June 1971.

THEMES

PSYWAR themes were central to all radio programs produced for VUNC. They stressed the following:

- The illegality of the North Korean action
- The fact that North and South Koreans are brothers
- That the real enemies are China and the Soviet Union
- That this is not the common man's war
- That the Communists cannot win against the world
- The exposure of the lies in NKPA/CCF propaganda
- Undistorted worldwide news
- Differences between life in the North and the South
- UN peace initiatives

Radio PSYWAR shared most of the themes the leaflet companies were using. It always had a double message, however, since both the North and South could tune in.

In all PSYWAR operations, good planning started with a clear understanding of the objectives established in Washington and at the PWS at FEC Headquarters. The next step was to get the message to the audience. Radio followed four precepts:

- Give the listener ample time to tune in, which means the broadcasting day must be of sufficient length, and broadcast on a regular schedule
- Make the message succinct, so even the surreptitious listener can hear all of it
- Permit repetition but avoid monotony
- Use material that is interesting to the listener

LANGUAGE PANELS

Panels reviewed the scripts and evaluated the presentation of radio broadcasts from the listeners' point of view. All the panels worked the same way.

For the VOA Mandarin review, the panel selected four recent programs that offered a variety of material and announcers. The panel consisted of eighteen native Mandarin speakers, divided into two groups of nine each. All were well educated and most had lived in the United States at one time or another. Ages ranged from the twenties to the sixties and members included students, teachers, scientists, and government workers. Apparently, no military personnel were selected. Many had recently arrived from China and were familiar with the types and styles of programs on Chinese radio.

The programs were played to each subpanel, then individuals were interviewed after each half hour. The researchers were interested in the panel members' impressions of the message, sentence structure, vocabulary, and program style. They noticed no glaring problems with the translations, but they complained that the style was too literary and stiff and that it sounded too formal and bookish. Too often, the script writers had used Western slang that could not be translated smoothly into Chinese, though the translators tried. The text was not in colloquial Chinese. They needed to mimic spoken syntax if they wanted to reach the common man.

The style of the broadcasts was also criticized. Too often, the announcers sounded like they were merely reading the script, which they were, rather than trying to sound spontaneous and natural. They sounded like dry speeches, which would quickly bore the Chinese audience. The announcer needed to talk to the listener.

In short, to make sure the common man would listen, the programs needed to be interesting and offer relief from the constant propaganda barrage from Radio Peking.[2]

1. Much of the information on VUNC and other Korean War radio stations is from Jerome K. Clauser's *Voice of the United Nations Command (VUNC): A Description of a Strategic Radio Broadcasting Psychological Operation* (US Army Research Organization, 1958). His report follows the history until the stations were closed and transferred to the South Koreans. Included are programming details and an analysis of the effectiveness of radio propaganda.

2. See William Daughtery's *Psychological Warfare Casebook* (Baltimore: Operations Research Office, Johns Hopkins, 1958) for a more in-depth discussion of the use of language panels and the Korean War experience with them.

5

Loudspeakers

In PSYWAR, loudspeakers are used for tactical propaganda. The theory for Korea was simple: Tailor a message for a particular audience for a specific time and use it in the battle area in close support of combat operations. In Korea, powerful loudspeakers were mounted on aircraft, and they broadcast surrender and other PSYWAR messages directly to enemy soldiers in the field. Loudspeakers were also mounted on jeeps and tanks for tactical uses. By order of a commanding general, the area where tactical PSYWAR could be used was limited to within forty miles of the battle front.

Effective use of loudspeakers depends on knowing to whom you are talking so that the message can be as personal as possible and in the listener's own dialect. Nothing could be more shattering to a unit than to have the enemy address soldiers by name and unit after they supposedly have been repositioned in secret. A typical announcement might be: "The people of Pak Sung welcome the soldiers of the 4th Regiment back to the war!" To prevent their men from hearing the loudspeakers, Communist officers would order them to fire their weapons, bang on empty containers, ring bells, and sing or shout.

The advantage of loudspeakers was that they could be brought close to the fighting where they could boom messages

National Archives

Meng Yuuhyon, a South Korean soldier attached to the 1st L&L, reads a surrender appeal to Chinese soldiers over a loudspeaker system, March 1952.

to the opposing forces, play nostalgic music—especially during holidays—and hide the movement of heavy equipment and tanks. Sometimes eerie noises were played to stimulate Oriental superstitions.

After the Inchon landing, UN forces rapidly pushed the NKPA out of South Korea and up the peninsula. The tactical loudspeaker equipment mounted on jeeps and tanks was not holding up. The mountainous terrain had few roads, and they were all very rocky. The loudspeaker equipment was too fragile to take the pounding. It was also not powerful enough to be heard over the battle, but larger, more powerful equipment would have been too cumbersome to follow the tactical battle line. Aircraft loudspeakers were suggested.

Aircraft had been outfitted with loudspeakers during World War II. The equipment was mounted on PV-1s, Navy aircraft, and then tested in North Africa, the Far East, and Europe. They were seldom used because the message could not be understood unless the plane flew slowly at less than 2,000 feet, making it an easy target. Later, the equipment was tried on Privateers, the Navy version of the Army's four-engined B-24 Liberator bomber. The Privateer could carry more electrical equipment, larger speakers, and defensive machine guns. The Privateers never made it to the theater before VJ Day, but the attempt was remembered by military planners.[1]

On 30 September 1950, the request for aircraft-mounted loudspeakers for Korea was sent to Washington. Two systems

A soldier of the 1st L&L sets up a loudspeaker system beamed at Chinese soldiers, March 1952.

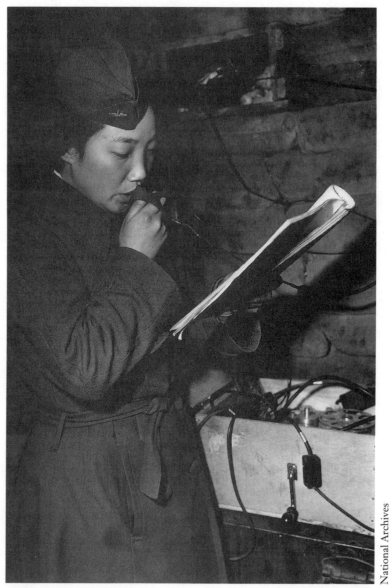

National Archives

Sergeant Kim Kwang Ja, a South Korean attached to the 1st L&L, broadcasts to NKPA troops, March 1953.

National Archives

Members of the 1st Loudspeaker Unit broadcast to the Chinese, who are dug in on a hill near Munye-ri, before UN troops move in. Private First Class Wilson drives the jeep while Sergeant O'Brien and Yang Yunn make the broadcast. Note the bullet holes in the windshield.

were located at a naval air station in California, and on 3 October, the equipment and several technicians landed in Korea. The equipment was immediately installed in the cargo door of a Gypsy C-47 and at 0230 hours on 8 October, the first loudspeaker mission took place, a test flight near Eighth Army Headquarters in Korea. The script was in Korean, but there were no Koreans on the ground to indicate if the message was understandable.

The next two missions were flown the following day over two battle area targets, again without verification that they were understood. The missions that followed tested the aircraft at 10,000 and 8,000 feet—altitudes at which it was impossible to hear the message. People on the ground said they heard something from the plane, but they couldn't understand the message.

By mid-March 1951, following strenuous requests from the Eighth Army, worthwhile aircraft loudspeaker tests were organized. Above 1,500 feet, the message was never understandable. The roar of the motors drowned out the speakers. The aircraft were tested at much lower altitudes, but even then the message was only understandable when the plane was directly overhead. The aircrew reported that the plane's equipment broadcast a very loud message, but those on the ground could barely hear it.

The equipment, with tube electronics, was of World War II vintage and was unreliable. Bad tubes and uncooperative generators were the major complaints. Intensive maintenance work helped to solve some of the problems. The loudspeakers themselves demanded close watching because they were sensitive to the vibrations and forces of flying. They could sound loud to the crew but not be delivering the volume they were designed to produce. The aircrew didn't have radio equipment for communicating with ground forces, so they never knew if the loudspeaker messages were being heard.

Two changes were suggested. First, the speakers were mounted underneath the aircraft so they could blare directly at the ground. The door-mounted speaker system did not work. Second, the aircraft were fitted with radios of the same type used by ground personnel so they could communicate with troops requesting Voice support.

Two of the aircraft assigned to the Special Air Missions detachment of the 21st Troop Carrier Squadron, the Kyushu Gypsies, were fitted with the high-power loudspeakers. They were designated "the Voice" and "the Speaker." The loudspeakers were first fitted to the cargo door, but later they were mounted in a custom unit on the belly of the C-47. The aircraft flew over enemy concentrations blaring PSYWAR messages about inferiority, surrender, death, frozen feet, and empty stomachs. The slow C-47s were obviously flying without fear, a visible testament to the Communists that their air force was ineffective. Ground fire was a continuing hazard because the Voice and Speaker aircraft often had to fly well under 5,000 feet to be heard.

DICK HUGHES, 21st TCS—Lieutenant Tom Minnow and I helped to prepare the first loudspeaker mission. I had been flying missions in Korea since 27 June 1950 and logged over 800 hours in the theater. When the CCF and NKPA surrounded the South Korean army, we first dropped surrender passes on them. Then we circled over them as low as we could without picking up too much ground fire and urged them over the loudspeakers to pick up the passes and surrender. The man on the mike was Paul Y Kim, a Chinese businessman from Hong Kong who was in Seoul on business when the war started and stayed to help the UN. We would leave the area, and the fighters would move in to drop napalm, et cetera. Then they left and we moved back over them so Paul could again urge them to use the passes or suffer the same treatment.

MARC MICHALAKES, 21st TCS—On a calm night, the sound could travel down from 8,000 feet AGL [above ground level]. But we generally flew the missions from approximately 2,000 to 4,000 feet AGL.

Airborne loudspeakers were often used by UN forces with female announcers to play off an Oriental prejudice. It was in-

National Archives

South Korean WACs attached to the Eighth Army PWS hook on their parachutes as a loudspeaker C-47 prepares to take off to broadcast surrender appeals to Communist troops, April 1952. The use of female voices was thought to have extra psychological impact. Note the leaflet bundles in the lower left, which would be thrown out before and after the loudspeaker broadcast.

sulting to the NKPA and CCF soldiers to have a "defenseless woman" fly over their lines with impunity. A woman's voice might also sound like the "woman they left behind." The Voice was credited with inducing more than 1,800 Chinese soldiers to surrender. The PSYWAR effect was most likely a cumulative one, and some credit for the surrenders must also be given to the battle situation.

The surrender messages were especially effective. In fact, a large group of Communist troops once surrendered to the circling SAM C-47 Voice plane, which then directed them where to walk. The C-47 was accompanied by four F-51s and the loudspeakers told the troops they would be napalmed if they didn't obey. More than 300 troops surrendered along with several trucks of supplies.

Of course, it was not easy for a Communist soldier to decide to surrender. He knew he would be shot if caught. He was also not sure of what awaited him. How would he communicate with the UN soldiers? Perhaps the UN soldiers couldn't be trusted and would shoot him as his officers had said they would. UN loudspeakers were used to counter these fears. Sometimes messages from captured CCF and NKPA soldiers

A South Korean soldier attached to the 1st L&L checks out her loudspeaker equipment before taking off over enemy territory, June 1952. She is seated in the jump seat of a B-26. No other records of B-26s with loudspeakers were found in Korean War documents.

were used to try to convince the soldiers that they could sur-render safely. UN artillery even laid smoke screens for them to run through. The loudspeakers announced the smoke before the barrage and then encouraged enemy soldiers to run.

OPERATION SLOWDOWN

OPERATION SLOWDOWN was a leaflet-loudspeaker ef-fort to maximize the effect of both on the enemy soldier. SLOWDOWN involved a series of eleven tapes of nostalgic music with Korean narration broadcast from the Voice aircraft and from jeeps, combined with several special leaflets. Some-thing similar had been tried earlier in an exercise called HAR-VEST MOON. Its purpose was to make enemy soldiers home-sick and lonely. The soldiers were encouraged to slow down and listen to the pleasant music. Then the narration would de-scribe things at home, the farms, the changing season. The message was nonpolitical and there were no surrender offers, but it was intended to make the Communist soldiers worry more about home and less about fighting.[2]

TALKING TANKS

"Talking tanks"—loudspeakers mounted on tanks—were de-veloped during World War II. The jeep was the most common loudspeaker vehicle, but it was totally unarmored and vulnera-ble to enemy fire. The tank offered considerable protection and could roll over terrain that would stop the jeep. The tank could follow the infantry advance over ditches, shallow rivers, and rough ground to stay close to the action, where tactical PSYWAR could do the most good. It could roll over and through enemy positions.

According to Elliot Harris, a typical tank loudspeaker script would be: "We are always ready to greet you with tor-rents of fire. It is impossible for you to succeed! Cease fighting now and save your life for your family." The tanks might play music, if so equipped, but generally they relied on live voice.

This M46 Patton tank is equipped with loudspeaker equipment and an auxiliary generator. The loudspeakers were unreliable because of the rough ride on the tank.

LEN MARTIN, Flame Plt, 1st Tank Bat, 1st Marine Div—While serving with the Flame Platoon in April '51, our flame tank [tank with a flame thrower] was pulled back to division HQ and assigned to work with an Army psychological warfare team. Over a period of a week or so, during which time we lived like kings, having no duties and having an Army lieutenant getting our mail, a loudspeaker was installed on our tank. The plan was to take the flame tank, with a North Korean prisoner inside, up to the front lines, demonstrate the effects of the flame thrower, and then have the prisoner encourage his compatriots to surrender.

1. See William Daughtery's *Psychological Warfare Casebook* and Robert Futrell's *The United States Air Force in Korea 1950–1953* for more information on the development of airborne loudspeakers.

2. Elliot Harris's *The "Un-American" Weapon* (New York: M. W. Lads, 1967) is perhaps the most thoughtful examination of the use of PSYWAR by the US government. It is recommended for those who desire an in-depth look into the ethical issues surrounding the use of psychological methods.

6

North Korean/Communist Chinese PSYWAR

The North Koreans and the Chinese, with some backing from the Soviet Union and the World Soviet, conducted their own PSYWAR operations.

The biggest psychological advantage the Communists had over UN troops was their fierce reputation. This was reinforced by their rapid advance down the Korean Peninsula after they crossed the parallel in 1950. The Inchon landing and the subsequent rapid retreat of the Communists to the Yalu River eliminated most of this advantage, but the addition of the Chinese troops reversed this trend. The retreat from the Yalu back to Seoul was devastating to UN morale after the liberation of almost all the peninsula.

The Chinese were ancient enemies of the Koreans and their military reputation had been inflated, despite their relative inferiority in resources and modern firepower. In battle, the CCF also proved to be tougher and more determined than many of the UN troops. Most of the UN troops were draftees who had no particular commitment to Korea, but the CCF troops were professional soldiers or draftees who would be quickly executed if they showed cowardice.[1]

JOHN SONLEY, 5th RCT—The question we asked ourselves was, "Why was the US here?" First of all, I was called back to active duty in September '51 from what I thought were the inactive reserves. I landed in Korea during the worst winter in recorded history. Never was I so cold, hungry, and miserable in my life, nor have I been since, even though I spent thirty-one years on the Chicago police force and was out in all kinds of weather and conditions. Korea wasn't our war. The Koreans had been under the control of someone else for years. I have always believed the politicians who are in favor of the war should be the ones to fight it. From both sides.

My main concern was, if hit, would I live or would I die? Would I lie on the battlefield and slowly bleed to death or even lose a limb? Another man and myself made an agreement that, should either of us be hit bad enough that the medic said there was no hope and would try to make death as comfortable as he could, the survivor would shoot the other.

When my unit took the ground at the 38th parallel, we all cheered as this meant that South Korea had been recovered, the ROK army could hold the line, and we could go home. When the word came for the line to continue north, many soldiers were unhappy, as there was not one reason for continuing the march. We had pushed the enemy across the 38th, which was the goal we had been told was the objective of the war.

After I found one of our men with his hands tied, shot under the chin and floating in the river, my attitude about the war changed a bit. Since I was forced to be there, kill them all and let's go home. About five men [UN soldiers] were found shot during that same day and, after that, any enemy soldier, hands up or down, was shot to death. No one in our sector would take prisoners until word came down that prisoners were needed for questioning.

Did I think it was a police action or that we belonged there? Did I care what happened to the land of Korea? Did I think anyone outside of Koreans should be dying for Korea? No.

COMMUNIST LEAFLETS

Communist leaflets were relatively rare, since they had few aircraft capable of delivering them to the front lines. Most Com-

Communist leaflets that were collected on Heartbreak Ridge in April 1952, one containing the name of a captured US Marine.

"*I Miss You So Much*"

This Communist leaflet is aimed at the homesick US soldier.

munist leaflets were delivered by artillery shell and Bedcheck Charlies—old, slow-flying aircraft used to harass UN troops— or left behind when a Communist unit abandoned its position to the UN forces. Sometimes CCF soldiers would crawl up to

UN outposts in the dark and leave cigarette lighters and leaflets, with booby traps, on the wires around the compound.

JOHN SONLEY, 5th RCT, M Company—I found my leaflets in a CCF position that they had just left. It was a court-martial offense to pick them up, but I did anyway and sent a few along to my mother and father. At the time, my father worked for the Chicago Tribune and he brought the leaflets to the editor of the paper, who reprinted them. A short time later, someone from the FBI came to the Tribune inquiring as to how the leaflets were obtained. They didn't tell them. My opinion at the time was that this was just some BS by the CCF. Our side had been feeding us BS all the time I was there.

I thought about keeping the surrender leaflet in case I ever became captured, which almost happened on 23 April '51. They were only 200 feet from us. They did not fire at us, nor we at them. As we left on our truck the CCF waved good-bye to us, perhaps because we were loading dead and wounded while throwing off 81mm mortar ammo.

The main target of the Communist leaflet campaign was US soldiers. The leaflets played on black-white racial tensions by using a picture of a black soldier being beaten by white military policemen. They tried to convince blacks that they were caught in a war started by white America. They included pictures of well-fed POWs to say it was better to be a POW than a soldier in the trenches. Often, the leaflets were ineffective because of the heavy political nature of the text, their poor and comical use of English, and the preposterous use of pictures from ads in *Life* magazine.

THE SOVIETIZATION OF KOREA

North Korea's plan for the peninsula after its victory was clearly based on Soviet and Stalinist principles of total control, with emphasis on the minds of the people to guarantee long-term conformance to the Communist ideal.[2] It used an unbreakable system of constant public indoctrination plus a ruthless policing system to keep the populace under control. In typical totalitarian style, it instituted a network of spies in every community it captured and organized "people's committees" to run things. People were shot by the police, but the violence was usually at night and seldom in the open.

Despite the police system, there were private conduits to pass on information and UN propaganda newspapers. An underground existed to help downed UN pilots and soldiers, and a black market was established to undermine North Korea's economy. Covert radios were tuned to UN broadcasts and the news passed via word of mouth through the villages, even though being caught with UN propaganda or a covert radio was a capital offense. Leaflets were the primary source of news, especially the larger news sheets, and peasants would brave Communist patrols to gather them at night.

Each time the Communists captured Seoul, they immediately began to operate Radio Seoul for their own purposes. The ROK did not destroy the equipment during its evacuation and the station, with its nationwide coverage, was captured intact. The Communists quickly began to broadcast that the South Korean government had fled and they were in control. "Go back to work," they said. "You work for us now." Personnel were brought from North Korean stations, including some Soviet-trained engineers. Former Radio Seoul personnel who stayed were pressed into Communist service and guaranteed fair treatment if they cooperated. All programs were written by trusted Communists from Radio Pyongyang.

Two newspapers, the *People's Daily News* and the *Liberation Daily News*, closed down by the ROK for their Communist leanings, were reopened and the publication of all other news-papers was stopped. The former Communist editors were reemployed. The only news service allowed was Tass from the Soviet Union. Like the radio station, the former ROK techni-cal personnel continued to run the presses, but the newspaper content was firmly controlled by the North Koreans.

The Communists also took over control of motion picture theaters. Western films were forbidden. Instead, theaters showed films selected for their ideological content. Admission was free to encourage good audiences at what were actually large indoctrination sessions. All able-bodied men who showed up at the theaters were conscripted into the NKPA. The movies had done the job of attracting men willing to hear the Communist line. Once they were all in the army, the theaters were closed.

Propaganda was centrally controlled to ensure that all forms of communication repeated the same themes. People were stopped in the street by the police and quizzed to see if they had remembered the message of the latest propaganda campaign. Often, they were expected to have memorized major sections. People who repeatedly refused to submit to this practice were "retired." The public was saturated at every turn with the Communist line through loudspeakers, radio pro-grams, newspapers, printed handbills, and textbooks in the schools. The loudspeakers continuously blared loud military and patriotic music.

Posters with simple slogans and pictures of Lenin, Stalin, Mao, and Kim Il Sung were plastered on every surface. They were attractively printed in bright colors, a strong contrast to the ubiquitous destruction of the war.

Communist infiltration even extended to the musical community in Seoul. The conductor of the symphony was forced to wear a military uniform and the name of the orches-tra was changed to the Red Army Chorus. The Communists "forgave" artists and musicians of their past opposition if they promised to contribute to the Communist system. By co-opting all popular art, music, drama, and other entertainment, the Communists had control of most avenues to the South Korean mind. Their long-term aim was to ensnare every aspect of Korean life in Communist doctrine. Though they occupied Seoul and South Korean villages only for short times, they were able to quickly establish their total control wherever they were.

PROPAGANDA THEMES

The social change instituted by the Communists during their three-month occupation of South Korea was based on five major propaganda themes designed to appeal to many Koreans and reinforced with a strenuous consolidation PSYWAR program of loudspeakers, posters, handbills, and forced-attendance lectures. There were two overall principles:

1. Every aspect of the consolidation program must be supported with a planned and deliberate PSYWAR program.

2. Propaganda must reflect long-range objectives and avoid easy short-range objectives if they differ from the long-range plan.

The five Communist PSYWAR themes were as follows:

1. The emancipation of women. The Communists made considerable political noise over their programs of rights for women. Divorce laws were redrawn to give the wife equal ownership of all property and, if she sued for divorce, she could claim all her husband's property. Legal prostitution was abolished. Women were brought into the political party system and given visible jobs in the Communist structure. The new rights were designed to open the work force to women. One of the most valuable resources of an underdeveloped country is a large, disciplined work force. Communists sought to add women to the industrial work force so men could be released to the army. There was no draft for women, though some voluntarily joined the NKPA. One of the effects of the new system

was to tear apart the South Korean family and replace it with the party. Posters proclaimed the role of women in the political future of a united Korea, but, as in the Soviet Union, the reality was more symbol than truth. Old-guard male Communists still held the power.

2. The emancipation of labor from capitalism. The labor program was most evident in the cities, where the industry was located. Not all industries were nationalized immediately, and small businesses were encouraged. Workers were promised shorter hours, a paid summer vacation at a government resort, paid sick leave, and a guaranteed rice ration. In reality, the paid vacations and sick leave and the expanded rice ration never happened. Hours were cut but were soon replaced with a quota production system that forced laborers to work until the quota was met, often longer than they were expected to work under the old system. In addition, workers were required to attend indoctrination lectures that only served to lengthen the already long workday. Small businesses were severely taxed, and raw material restrictions forced many to close. Because the Communists never delivered on their propaganda promises, the workers became very disillusioned.

3. Youth program. There was a strenuous program to recruit and convert young men and women to Communism. The Political Democratic Youth organization was instituted as a starting point for party membership. The young people were promised expanded opportunities for education and social advancement no matter what their former economic status. Literacy was to be achieved by a system of universal education. Exceptional students could look forward to a free university education, possibly in China or even the Soviet Union. The biggest obstacle for this program was a lack of teachers. Many teachers had been forced onto labor gangs because they were judged to be politically unreliable. Some progress was made against illiteracy, but people were taught only words and concepts that fit the political system, not the things of value to a

merchant, teacher, or professional. So the education system became a political indoctrination factory. The high schools also became a hunting ground for the draft. Male students in their early teens could find themselves in the army and then on the front lines in less than a week.

4. Redistribution of land. The redistribution of farmland was to be based on the number of people living in a household. Each farmer was to get his fair share, which appealed to the formerly landless peasant class, who had worked as sharecroppers and didn't own their crops. Land was taken from land owners without compensation, but the peasant farmers to whom it was allotted had to pay the government for their share plus a 25 percent tax based on their annual yield. When the North Korean government instituted special levies for war costs, the actual tax was closer to 75 percent. Farmers were also expected to house and feed soldiers in their barns without compensation. The land redistribution program, popular at first, rapidly lost its appeal.

5. Nationalism and the Communist ideal. The propaganda line of "Korea for the Koreans" was relentless and expressed in all the media. The line was impossible to escape because it was part of every facet of life. Popular national myths and heroic figures were modified to serve the Communist propaganda call. People were constantly bombarded with slogans and songs about the imperialist Americans and the oppressive and corrupt South Korean government. The assistance of the United Nations by Japan, an ancient Korean enemy, was assailed as a continuation of its oppression. Many of these themes were favorably received by the populace because they were easy to believe. For example, South Korean officials were known to have lined their pockets with public money.

The Communists wanted their people to believe the United Nations would never force the North Koreans to retreat. The rapid advance of the North Koreans had proven that the United States was weak and would never rescue the South. Initially the Soviets were hailed as the fathers of Korean Communism, but this line was deleted because Koreans saw them as outsiders. The ideology campaign, though successful at first, was perverted by the oppressive political control of the Communist government. People who had been drawn in by the early consolidation PSYWAR of the Communists became disillusioned and grew to hate the harsh actions of the government. Overt resistance was out of the question because of the danger. Covert activity was difficult, but it happened. Freedom of thought was just as difficult.

CHESTER BAIR, 34th Heavy Tank Co, 7th Inf Div— When the Chinese got into the war, they would gather the women, children, and old people together and give them drugs and speeches. They told them we are here to fight for you, but you must help. If you do not do as ordered, you will be killed as a traitor. Then they would force them to attack UN forces. They came screaming at us and we in turn did not want to shoot at them, especially the South Korean soldiers, because these were their families. After these "assault forces" went through your positions, then came the Chinese. We tried to zigzag our tank when they attacked us so we wouldn't hurt any. Sometimes the Chinese would hide in the crowd and fire on us, so we had to fire on them. The Chinese would attack when we were needing to regroup and also needing ammo. This hurt morale for all UN forces.

CAMPFIRES

When the Chinese entered the war in November 1950, UN intelligence officers were unsure how many divisions had been committed. The Chinese did all they could to further the confusion. Before 2 December 1950, UN night intruder flights rarely reported more than a half-dozen campfires in the hills occupied by the Communists, who clearly wanted to remain hidden despite the cold of winter. Suddenly, after 2 December, the pilots reported seeing hundreds, maybe thousands, of campfires covering the hills, like they were ablaze. But how many troops were really there?

The Chinese deception had solid PSYWAR roots. The plan was that a large number of campfires would lead UN intelligence to overestimate the number of Chinese troops in North Korea and cause the United Nations to redeploy forces against a phantom enemy. If it looked like a strong Chinese force, this would cause the UN troops to fear defeat and would lower their morale. It was an effective act. The UN command was struck by the possibility that there were more Chinese than it had initially thought.

RADIO PROPAGANDA

North Koreans used radio propaganda to disguise their war plans. A week before they crossed the parallel into South Korea in 1950, Radio Pyongyang broadcast a call for open elections over the entire peninsula—a delay tactic. Several days later, North Korea announced by radio an offer to have a meeting with the United Nations and South Korean political parties at a site on the parallel. In reality, the NKPA planned to cross the parallel, which they soon did. A radio broadcast was again used to announce that South Korea had attacked first.

Later in the war, radio was used by the NKPA to broadcast false peace offerings in an attempt to cause indecision and hesitation in the UN command. Often, these broadcasts were reported to originate from the "Central Peace Commission" or a similarly legitimate-sounding group.

Even though they were virtually absent from the sky, the Communists continually boasted about their aerial victories. They used Radio Pyongyang to glorify their successes. Two pilots, "Hero Kim" and "Hero Ong," showed up in several broadcasts. These and other pilots were reputed to have shot down dozens of aircraft. One of these pilots was later shot down in his ancient YAK fighter by an F-84, but no mention of his passing was made on Radio Pyongyang. The broadcasts were intended to hurt the morale of the South Korean air force while bolstering that of the northerners. Over the span of the war, the numbers of UN aircraft reportedly shot down added up to an impressive total; the Communists destroyed the UN air force several times over!

Propaganda broadcasts were carefully staged. The NKPA produced authentic-sounding stories from reporters on the scene and interviews with victims, claiming massacres by UN forces. The NKPA boasted about their victories and expressed "sorrow" for UN losses. They daily announced their own attacks, giving false information, and claimed they would drive UN forces into the sea.

BEDCHECK CHARLIE

It's a Korean War cliché. The GIs are asleep in their tents. At midnight, a lone aircraft flies overhead, its engine intentionally misfiring to create a racket. Everyone wakes up and runs for shelter because sometimes these guys carry small bombs or drop grenades and artillery shells. One of the biggest threats is not from the enemy, but from falling antiaircraft shells, so everyone wants to hit the shelter. The aircraft also drops PSYWAR leaflets. He causes a commotion and leaves, the engine droning off into the distance, unseen in the dark. The GIs have just been visited by Bedcheck Charlie, a.k.a. Pisscall Pete.[3]

Bedcheck Charlie raids were never a real military threat to UN forces. They weren't much of a psychological threat, either. The UN command took them seriously, however, since there were a limited number of F-86 Sabres in the theater and it was worried that a single attack could destroy many of the fighters allotted to the Korean theater. The Bedcheck Charlies had to be stopped. At the most, they were a possible threat to

Steven Rook

Bedcheck Charlie often used a Polikarpov PO-2, a type of aircraft that dated from the late 1920s.

life. At the least, they were colorful and amusing, and they afforded everyone a chance to visit the loo.

Bedcheck Charlies operated throughout the Korean War, but their use increased during the last six months, when the front lines were static. They used the Sariwon airfield, unserviceable except for slow propeller aircraft, and informal airfields and roads. Their attacks were often just after midnight, hence the nickname. The North Koreans primarily used the Polikarpov PO-2, a Soviet-built biplane dating from 1927, and the Yakolev YAK-18, a low-wing aircraft of more recent vintage but with no better performance. On one occasion, they even flew the Blochavidan MBE-2, a pusher-type seaplane that looked like a prop from a World War I movie. The PO-2 and YAK-18 cruised at less than 90 mph, too slow for UN jets to shoot down. The Soviets used the same planes during World War II as liaison and ambulance aircraft, and as night raiders.[4]

The pilots often made their old radial engines growl and pop loudly to harass UN troops. The PO-2 was nearly invisible to radar because of its all-wood construction. It took off from unprepared grass fields close to the front and flew low to further reduce the probability of detection. The air defense systems around Seoul, code named Dentist, usually picked up the intruders, but the detection hits were so spotty that few definitive tracks could be formed.

MARION WILLIAMS, 21st TCS—The last time Kimpo was retaken, we were stationed there. Every night, a little plane, a crop duster type, would come over and cause everyone to head for the slit trenches. In due time, we put up antiaircraft guns, one of them a 40mm gun just outside our tent. They couldn't use fighter planes, as none could fly slow enough to get behind the troublesome little guy. The problem was that antiaircraft crews couldn't fire until they were given permission. One night, the warning sounded and we all stood outside to watch him fly over in the bright moonlight. The gun crew never got permission to fire. After that, I don't think anyone got up when the warning sounded.

Sometimes flying in groups of two or three, as opposed to the usual single aircraft, the Charlies headed for UN airfields, troop positions, combat headquarters, or any target that looked good to the pilot. On 13 October 1952 (and at least three times later), up to four PO-2s raided the UN Search and Rescue air base on Cho-do Island, dropping the usual small bombs and strafing targets, including the radar facility. On 28 November, an aircraft dropped several small fragmentation bombs on the F-51 Mustangs of the 8th Fighter Bomber Group at Pyongyang Airfield, damaging three so severely that they were never flown again. One American sergeant was killed and several other soldiers were wounded.

In a side note, the investigation after the raid found six

Korean laborers nearby carrying Chinese papers. One of them carried papers identifying him as a captain in the CCF!

The heckling caused little damage but stirred great concern within the UN air defense system. Antiaircraft guns were in short supply, as were radar units and defense aircraft. Defenses often were only searchlights and automatic weapon teams. Late in the war, small gap-filler radar units became available to cover valley approaches.

Even with radar protection, airfields were vulnerable. Jet-capable airfields were rare close to the battle lines, so they were crowded. Fighters that are parked dangerously close together make easy targets. Gas and ammunition were stored in huge dumps that were only lightly defended. If the Communists had ever mounted a real air attack, Seoul and many military areas would have been at risk. Another early PO-2 attack came against the airfield at Suwon. It was recorded in the diary of one of the pilots, La Woon Yung. The airfield, home to the 335th Fighter Squadron's F-86s, feared no attacks and was well lit. The PO-2s dropped two small bombs each, destroying a Sabre and severely damaging four.

> **DICK HUGHES,** 21st TCS—Bedcheck Charlie—Piss-call Pete, as we called him—would putt-putt over our tents at Kimpo around 2 A.M. on his way to Suwon just south of us. He was a two-seat trainer with open cockpits. The man in the back threw out mortar shells along the way, and he was successful in destroying an F-86 at Suwon one morning. Was later shot down north of Seoul.

As the truce talks intensified toward the end of spring 1953, so did the nuisance flights. On 26 May, at least six PO-2s dropped small bombs and artillery shells on the K-14 airfield near Inchon, setting a gas pipeline on fire. Less than a week later, Bedcheck Charlies attacked the K-6 airfield, more than fifty miles behind the lines. K-6 jet fighters, mostly lined up in vulnerable rows, were perfect targets for the little bombs, but there was no damage to them from this attack.

Groups of Charlies attacked Seoul on 8 June, killing several people and injuring several dozen. This raid was particularly bold in that one apparent target was President Syngman Rhee's residence, though it wasn't hit. A week later, a petroleum dump near Inchon was bombed by PO-2s. It burned for days, consuming more than 50,000 gallons of gasoline. Air defenses tried to locate the slow aircraft with searchlights, and shells peppered the sky, but no aircraft were downed.

Though jet fighters could not counter the Charlies, a few T-6 Mosquitoes worked with a C-47 Firefly (flare) aircraft in the hope of seeing the attackers, without immediate success. Several PO-2s were shot down by a B-26 and a Navy F7F Tiger Cat, but the Charlies were so slow that they could maneuver sharply away from most attacks and disappear by flying very low to the ground.

In an effort to stop the night raiders, on 10 June 1953, B-29s started daily attacks on the fifteen or so airfields just across the battle lines. They cratered the runways and destroyed every piece of ground equipment they could find, and Fifth Air Force Sabres strafed the fields. The heckling continued, but at a lower level. Apparently, the rugged PO-2s and YAK-18s could still find sufficient space for takeoff, perhaps from roads or fields.

The Navy decided that a squadron of propeller-driven Corsair fighters of World War II vintage might be the answer. Each carrier assigned two Corsairs to the night fighter squadron based at K-6, thirty-five miles south of Seoul. After a week's instruction in night fighting, they were sent against the raiders. Lieutenant Bordelon shot down two Charlies, probably YAK-18s, on 29 June 1953. The next evening, he shot down two more, either LA-9s or 11s. He was awarded the Silver Star with a Gold Star, indicating a dual award. VADM

J. J. Clark, commander of the Seventh Fleet, promised that anyone shooting down five raiders would earn the Navy Cross. On 18 July, ten days before the armistice, Lieutenant Guy Bordelon shot down his fifth Bedcheck Charlie, another YAK-18, and VADM Clark awarded him the medal. Bedcheck Charlie flights dwindled to nothing because of the success of the Corsairs, B-29s, and Sabres. Lieutenant Bordelon was the only naval fighter ace of the war.[5]

SHOUTS, SMOKE BOMBS, AND INSULTS

Chinese soldiers were noted for talking and shouting to UN forces during an attack and at night. They would scream threats and insults in bad English and call to their South Korean "brothers." The Communists favored night attacks, especially when there was at least a partial moon. Imagine the terror of having thousands of enemy soldiers running toward you, barely seen, if at all, in the dark, and all of them yelling and screaming as their artillery shells begin to land. It was a surreal and nightmarish experience.

Infantry attacks were often preceded by heavy artillery barrages to soften up enemy positions, and the same tactic of advancing with screams and yells during the artillery barrage was used. Certainly the Communist soldiers took horrible losses, but apparently it was worth the appearance of invulnerability and fanaticism. The Communists were also known to advance behind a shield of South Korean prisoners or villagers, including women and children.

The Communists favored moving their troops at night, sometimes by mule, but such movements were noisy, even when moving a few men. They covered up the noise with false activity in their former location. They would leave men to talk loudly, ring cowbells, and blow whistles and bugles. These noises meant the enemy was on the move and men in the UN outposts hated to hear them.

MARION WILLIAMS, 21st TCS—After the Marines went ashore at Wonson, our flight was attached to them to air-supply units cut off in the mountains. After Wonson was evacuated, we moved farther north to Hamhung. The Army unit that was defending the field had to be resupplied several times. Their positions were just outside the building we were sleeping in. Like an old World War II infantryman, I went out at night and talked to the guys in the positions. The Communists played mind games every night. A light would flash, then another. A whistle would blow, then another. A horn someplace else. The guys said this happened every night, usually before they attacked. This night, they never attacked, but they kept everyone on edge all night.

CHESTER BAIR, 34th Heavy Tank Co, 7th Inf Div— I entered the war 16 September 1950. We fought our way to South Mountain, Seoul, South Korea. Afterwards, we went to North Korea and were at the Chosin Reservoir when the Chinese entered the war. The Chinese would blow horns and use colored smoke bombs, often as signals to their troops, but they sent us a message as well. One horn they used sent chills down your back, I don't care how brave you were.

They used three colors of smoke bombs: yellow, blue, and green. When the Chinese used these bombs, it caused a reaction from their troops; green and they would attack. You never knew for sure what they meant, so this caused a lot of rumors among our troops. We, in turn, would use our own colored smoke bombs to try and confuse the enemy. This worked, but it confused us, too, and made us afraid [since it may have sent an unwanted message] because they outnumbered us in most cases.

They also used horns and bugles. These I believe they used for commands to their troops. It made you afraid because you knew they were up to something again, and not for your best interest. One horn they would play at night had a sound that turned your blood cold. I always thought it was steam powered, it lasted so long, but one could make the same noises on a violin. It was really like a long, low, off-key chord on the violin. It was the noise one would expect to hear in a cemetery at night.

LOUDSPEAKERS

The Chinese didn't often use their loudspeakers until the front lines stagnated in 1952. Then they broadcast music and long lectures about how this was not a US war. Some of the music was nostalgic, making the soldiers think about home. Other music taunted UN troops or boasted about Communist power. In the lectures, the UN troops were urged to go home. In a demonstration of their intelligence gathering, their loudspeakers welcomed new UN units as they arrived, even if the troop movement was supposed to be a secret.

EDWARD HANRAHAN, 3rd Inf Div, 15th Inf Reg, Co B—I never heard their bugles, but I remember hearing loudspeakers playing music. I think the song was "When the Moon Comes over the Mountain."

GERMS

One propaganda tactic used by the Communist news media was to claim that the United Nations was using germ warfare in Korea. The claims were backed by signed confessions from captured US pilots, and world health organizations reported that there were epidemics in some North Korean cities. Were we spreading typhus and bubonic plague? What was the truth?[6]

False claims of germ warfare were an established Communist PSYWAR tactic by the time the Korean War began. The Soviets had made similar claims during World War II against the Germans, and Stalin even used "evidence" of germ warfare against his political rivals during the purges in the 1930s. Post–World War II Communist propaganda continued to use the germ warfare theme, claiming that the United States was using Eskimos and Indians in experiments. Crop failures were blamed on CIA balloons that dropped potato bugs and lice.

Korean germ warfare accusations started in February 1952 and increased soon after the United Nations began to push the Communists back into North Korea late that year and again after the POW riots at Koje-do.

The claims may have been partially based on the Communists' genuine fear. During World War II, the Japanese ran a special prison camp in China called Unit 731.[7] They experimented with bacteriological warfare on US, British, Soviet, and Chinese POWs and investigated the use of insects as a carrying agent. The Japanese scientists disappeared after the war. Several may have been tried and executed by the Soviets. The Chinese thought the United States had taken the scientists into custody because of their advanced knowledge of germ warfare and its effects. Perhaps the United States, guided by its Camp 731 data, was trying bugs on the Chinese again.

Chinese propagandists circulated photos of special germ hunters poking around supposed infected areas with chopsticks, looking for special flies the United States had developed to carry disease to North Korea. North Korean propaganda even claimed that the United States had developed a special species of housefly that was resistant to the sub-zero Korean winter. Epidemics in the war zone caused by poor health care and filthy conditions were claimed to be the result of germs dropped by UN aircraft. The Communists energized their own branches of the Red Cross to seek outside verification of the epidemics, which they did, but germ warfare could not be identified as the cause.

The germ warfare battle heated up when the Communists began to extort "confessions" from captured UN airmen. The Communists filmed and recorded the confessions of Air Force and Marine airmen. They signed the papers after many months of interrogation and were undoubtedly forced into the confessions. Over a grueling ten-day period in early 1953, the men were interviewed by Communist and Western journalists and "scientists" who were sympathetic to the Communist line. The Communist propaganda machine had an enormous volume of material to work with, ranging from tape recordings to a long propaganda movie of the event.

The confessions were amazingly detailed. The POWs revealed their flight routes, complete descriptions of their air-crafts' special biological modifications, and histories of their assignments. The confessions often were more than thirty minutes long and always included political statements unchar-acteristic of the confessor. According to the confessions, the United States was desperate because of Communist successes in the war and was using these illegal measures to turn the tide.[8]

To substantiate the claims, the Communists instituted a nationwide inoculation campaign and published "scientific" papers from their ministries of agriculture and health. The Chinese claimed the United States was routinely flying sorties over the mainland to sow diseased bugs and germs, though they never produced any convincing evidence. They claimed the United States dropped deadly grasshoppers, poisoned food, tainted toothpaste, excrement, and dead and decaying birds and animals in the effort to infect North Korea. The organisms were reportedly delivered in special germ-proof planes in bomblike containers from bases in Japan and Okinawa.

Requests by the Red Cross and the World Health Organization to inspect the epidemic areas were refused. The Communists sponsored tours for selected journalists to targeted areas where peasants talked about their germ experiences. A germ warfare exhibit was established in Peking for the world press that included material from the confessions, preserved insects, and other physical "proof." Communist members of the United Nations began to demand that the General Assembly order the attacks stopped. Communist organizations around the world were energized to demonstrate and riot to protest UN germs. There were protest rallies in Western Europe. The claims were so convincing that the rallies were sponsored by peace groups that had no ties to Communist organizations. It was a well-orchestrated propaganda effort.

If nothing else, the germ warfare campaign helped to generate considerable anti-US and anti-UN hatred among the common people in North Korea. Downed allied airmen were in genuine danger from peasants who were convinced the planes were sowing disease and death on them. The germ campaign also served the cause of Communist propaganda around the world. Americans were called "New Nazis" and the United States was said to be run by "Chicago gangsters."

It was relatively easy for the Communists to make propaganda use of UN prisoners. They often carried personal papers from which their signatures could be copied. This always made a confession with a signature suspect. And, as General Mark Clark said in his memoir, there was something to fear in the germ warfare propaganda campaign. It was possible that the

Communists were using this PSYWAR onslaught to establish the legitimacy of a counterattack, a genuine germ and chemical campaign.

The germ warfare claims were unsubstantiated. They were a second front for the Communists, another theater in which to conduct war, a diversion from their own troubles. But, did the Communists have their own germ warfare program, one that the United States knew about but kept secret?

WARREN HARPER, Reg Recon Plt, 187th RCT— During November 1950, we were sent out on a patrol north of Pyongyang to investigate an alleged North Korean professor who was experimenting with mice. We found the place, destroyed the mice, all the lab equipment, et cetera; not a shot was fired. Things were pretty hush-hush. I forgot about the event, until I read that the lieutenant in charge got the Silver Star. First thing that went through my mind was, a Silver Star when not a shot was fired?

The US reaction to the accusations and confessions was an official silence, which in 20/20 hindsight may have been wrong. Certainly, the UN command was shocked by the claims. The radio confessions by the aviators were greatly disturbing to the United States. It was also thought that issuing a comment on the claims would lend them too much credibility. The silence was meant to be an arrogant refusal to recognize the claims, but the world thought it was embarrassed shock at having been discovered. Communist PSYWAR naturally tried to reinforce this impression. The United Nations finally produced a leaflet in Korean denying the charges and suggesting that the epidemics were due to poor sanitation.

1. *Public Opinion Quarterly*, page 69, and *Psychological Warfare Casebook*, pages 482–85.

2. See Daughtery's *Psychological Warfare Casebook* for several studies relating to the treatment of conquered territory by the NKPA and CCF. The articles examine the system of control the Communists instituted over civilians and the psychological methods that helped make it work.

3. For an entertaining discussion of the Bedcheck Charlie flights, see Robert Futrell's *The United States Air Force in Korea 1950–1953*.

4. The PO-2 was typical of that era in aviation development. It had two open cockpits, fixed landing gear, and no real armament. It looked like an old crop duster and was, in fact, used as such. The five-cylinder air-cooled engine could barely pull the plane past ninety mph. Most flights loped along at about seventy.

5. The best account of the Navy's actions against the Bedcheck Charlie flights is in Commander Malcolm W. Cagle and Commander Frank A. Manson's *The Sea War in Korea* (Annapolis, MD: US Naval Institute, 1957).

6. For an interesting contrast, look at the germ warfare discussions in Joseph C. Goulden's *Korea: The Untold Story of the War* (New York: Times Books, 1982), and Elliot Harris's *The "Un-American" Weapon*.

7. Callum MacDonald shows how Camp 731, Korean germ warfare, and the Panmunjom peace talks were linked in *Korea: The War before Vietnam*. Also see Peter Williams and David Wallace, *Unit 731: Japan's Secret Biological Warfare in WWII* (New York: The Free Press, 1989).

8. See Harris's *The "Un-American" Weapon* for discussions on the germ warfare confessions.

7

Prisoners of War

PRISONERS HELD BY UN FORCES

By early 1951, the United Nations held nearly 140,000 North Korean and 20,000 Chinese POWs. General Ridgway thought they posed a security threat if left close to the front, so all POWs were eventually transported to Koje-do, a small island south of mainland South Korea. The prison compounds that the Army built were not large enough to hold that many prisoners, so they were dangerously overcrowded. Because good soldiers were needed to fight the war, the South Korean army posted its poorest soldiers as guards, and the US Army assigned few personnel. The NKPA and CCF considered the prisons extensions of the battlefield. They infiltrated the prisons and began to organize. The overcrowding was just the igniter of conflict and unrest that they needed.

The CCF organized a security unit within the camp to maintain discipline among the prisoners and to limit cooperation with the guards. The NKPA trained soldiers to be prison camp leaders and allowed them to be captured, knowing all roads led to Koje-do Island. The security unit in the camp instituted a propaganda campaign to correct the prisoners' thoughts and to ensure belief in the ultimate Communist victory. POWs who were slow to "learn" were often beaten by the security unit members and some were killed. In Compound 62, where CCF discipline was especially tight, the prisoners erected a statue of Stalin and a Communist flag. The overcrowded conditions, the inadequate number of prison guards, and the resulting lack of control allowed for this type of display.

When truce negotiations began in early 1952, one of the first topics was the return of POWs. The United Nations was interested in settling this quickly because of the logistic burden the POWs represented, and it began to interrogate POWs on Koje-do in preparation for repatriation. Any who wanted to remain in the South could be exploited for propaganda purposes. When UN interrogators arrived at Compound 62, POWs met them with clubs and other improvised arms. The nervous UN troops opened fire, killing 77 POWs and wounding more than 140.

Communist newspapers and radio broadcasts called the incident a massacre and a war crime of the highest proportions. The POWs signed petitions in their own blood asking for humane treatment and continued their psychological battle with the guards. The Communist radio claimed the POW actions were just those of men who desperately wanted to return home. The POWs and their guards were at a stalemate. The UN prison authorities didn't enter the camp. They were stopped by the aggression of the NKPA and CCF prisoners. The Communist POW leadership wanted unconditional repatriation without any opportunity for CCF or NKPA soldiers to opt to stay in the South. POWs with a desire to stay were killed to deter other POWs from making the same choice. The PSYWAR battle was carried by China to the international press: "The UN is making unreasonable demands on Communist POWs and won't let them come home. Communist POWs want to return to the worker's paradise rather than stay in the decadent South." Another claim of the unrest was to force the UN to take combat troops away from the front lines in order to restore order to the camp compound.

Truce negotiators asked for a final screening of the prisoners and for the repatriation, which had begun at other camps, to continue. Of the 160,000 POWs on Koje-do, only 70,000 wanted to return to the North. Many said that they preferred to stay in the South and would violently resist repatriation. Some must have been agents looking to infiltrate South Korea, but most were thought to be honest. This was a considerable loss of face for the Communists and truce talks were suspended.

When the talks resumed in April 1952, the Communist negotiators demanded that all Communist prisoners, regardless of disposition, be returned, by force if necessary, to the North before any further negotiations could proceed. This meant that more than 130,000 POWs would be repatriated. The Communists were willing to leave only the former ROK soldiers that had been pressed into their service. Truman refused to negotiate with human beings and the talks recessed again.

Meanwhile, the POWs in Compound 62 had captured General Francis Dodd, the commandant of the camp, who had gone to them to negotiate the stalemate. General Clark, the commander of UN forces in Korea, prepared to do whatever was necessary to regain control of the camp.

Eventually, a show of force by General "Bull" Boatner won General Dodd's release. Boatner was then appointed as the new commander of the camp. Several more riots ensued, but Boatner, with a firm show of strength, gradually reestablished control. No prisoners from the camp were exchanged until very late in the war, and the Communist radio propaganda assault asserting claims of mistreatment continued.

PRISONERS HELD BY THE COMMUNISTS

The Communist prisons, especially those in the North, were hard to recognize as such. There was little wire and few guards. There was no need for any. UN POWs were easily identified as non-Koreans, and with miles of frozen, barren hills in every direction and no neutral country to run to, as there was in Europe in World War II, escape was not practical.

The Communists concealed several of their POW camps, despite legal requests for their location. The camps may have been in urban areas, and the UN forces needed to know where not to bomb. Through careful intelligence gathering and interrogation of POWs, the probable locations of all the camps were eventually determined.

Chinese prisons were worse than those run by the North Koreans. Prisoners were beaten, thrown into latrine pits, and subjected to harsh interrogations. They were threatened with death, and mock executions were held.[1]

When a UN soldier was taken prisoner, he was first interrogated to determine his "value." Communist interrogators looked for high-ranking officers or for soldiers who held jobs in intelligence, logistics, and operations who could make credible "confessions." The common soldier often had little information and he was either shot, especially if wounded, or quickly sent to a prison camp. There, additional interrogation would determine who might break or be susceptible to more intense methods. These men were then singled out to be developed into a PSYWAR asset—examples of the oppressed American.

Valuable prisoners, such as pilots and high-ranking officers, were separated for further questioning by professionals. They were given a friendly reception and asked to fill out a questionnaire in order to register their capture with the Red Cross. In reality, the questionnaire was just the first step in the process to determine what they knew and who was weak. Some received tougher treatment than others. They were deprived of food, water, and warmth; left outside to sleep in a muddy hole; and threatened with execution and torture. Information from the questionnaire and other interrogation was slowly exploited.

Selected prisoners were lectured day and night on Communist theory and other propaganda. They were given tests without warning and were expected to answer questions on the lectures. Wrong answers resulted in beatings, and if they resisted, the beatings were tougher. Often groups of prisoners were punished for the resistance of one member. One method used to increase the psychological pressure was to keep the prisoners from establishing a predictable routine. A prisoner could wait, standing in an anteroom, for hours for his interrogation. He could be roused at night or every half hour around the clock for short interrogation sessions.

Prisoners were encouraged to write home, but the letters were scrutinized by the interrogators for clues as to lines of questioning. Incoming letters were screened. Those with bad news or other information that had negative psychological value were passed on to the POW or read to the entire group. Other mail was held up or destroyed and the prisoner was told that the lack of mail was due to the indifference of his family and friends. All these tactics combined to decrease the POW's ability to resist and increase his willingness to cooperate. Some who broke under interrogation signed petitions or other fairly unimportant pieces of paper. They were rewarded with cigarettes, medical care, warmer clothing, and better food. Men accepting even small rewards would be more vulnerable to greater pressure later on.

It's generally thought that POWs who signed the petitions were doing so out of ignorance or cowardice, but there were other reasons for cooperating. Because the POWs were isolated and their mail was often withheld, they were unsure if their relatives knew whether they were dead or alive. By signing a petition, which the Communists would surely release to the press, a prisoner could let his family know that he was well enough to at least write. Also, if a prisoner's name appeared in print or if he appeared in a newsreel or on the radio, the Communists could not deny that he had been a prisoner. If he were recognized as a POW, they would have to free him at the end of the war.

Hard cases were treated very harshly. Persistently un-cooperative prisoners were classified as not worth the effort and sent to a camp where they were no longer exploited.[2] A group of prisoners with a solid group identity that survived despite all efforts to destroy it was also separated from more vulnerable POWs. There were enough easier targets to consider. Because group solidarity among US prisoners was reputed to be low, nearly 38 percent of US POWs died in captivity and several chose to stay in North Korea after the armistice. By comparison, the small group of Turks, soldiers with a very tough reputation who had solid group discipline and support, survived their captivity without one fatality or defection.

CHESTER BAIR, 34th Heavy Tank Co, 7th Inf Div— When the Chinese would close in, some UN forces would drop their weapons, place their hands over their heads, and walk towards the enemy. That's why many POWs don't like to talk about capture. I was captured three times in one day, 1 December '50, but I escaped each time. This happened east of the Chosin Reservoir. My Army unit was wiped out that day. We were mostly with our vehicles on the road while the Chinese commanded the high ground around us. We were outnumbered ten to one.

At the Chosin Reservoir, I drove a truckload of supplies, C rations, and small arms ammo. Soon my truck became a hearse, then loaded with wounded. The Chinese took over the convoy piece by piece. As they did, they would set fire to the trucks still loaded with the wounded and dead. The soldiers I saw surrender were men that had had no sleep for four nights, some no food or drink. All they had was the snow on the ground to eat. They saw dead and wounded all around them; some were without ammo and were too exhausted to resist. Some sat down and refused to move until the Chinese overran their positions. Most of them were wounded. But whatever the reason, the fight was out of them, so they quit. I believe that with what they saw and had endured they reached a breaking point.

In Vietnam, helicopters took the men into combat, supplied them with whatever they needed, and removed the wounded and supplied the replacements. The soldiers saw this and it helped the morale. They could expect attention and care most of the time they were in combat. This was not so in Korea. At the Chosin Reservoir, we knew there was no one on either flank, they were not removing our wounded, nor were they bringing in replacements, and very few supplies got to us. We did not get a combat rescue team as we thought, and this was a great morale breaker as well. So after you have all these things happen, you lose heart.

Radio Confessions

The most devastating use of POWs was in Communist radio propaganda. They were coerced, some within just a few days of capture, to make outlandish confessions of hospital bombings, germ warfare, and other war crimes against the North Koreans. Actually, the UN forces were operating under very strict rules and were not allowed to strike military targets that were within range of sensitive civilian targets. Nevertheless, the radio confessions were almost impossible to discredit, and some doubt would always remain.

To the Western world, the radio confessions were graphic evidence of the brutality of the war and the enemy. It was impossible to imagine what tactics the Communists were using to persuade POWs to confess on the radio to false and illegal military operations like germ warfare. Some POWs undoubtedly were seeking favorable treatment in the prison camp or were naively tricked into making what they thought were innocent recordings. Some, however, had obviously been converted by Communist indoctrination and were collaborating willingly. Twenty-one US POWs refused to be repatriated after the armistice, and the US public and soldiers in Korea were haunted by thoughts of what the Communists must have done to get their sons, fathers, and friends to switch sides.

Communist leaflets and press releases announced when US POWs would be interviewed on Radio Peking. There were three regular interview sessions on the Communist radio, at 0730, 1800, and 2230 every Tuesday and Friday. The interviews were sponsored by the Chinese Peace Committee, a front organization for the Communist Party.

The Communists also made considerable propaganda and psychological use of notable Westerners whom they invited to North Korea. The visitors were paraded before movie cameras and press photographers. They made statements contrary to the stated policy of the United Nations and United States and so created the impression that the world was not united against North Korea. This was a significant PSYWAR victory for the Communists, and they used it in their propaganda and against UN POWs.

The theory that UN prisoners were "brainwashed" has been discredited. What did happen was that the Communists used strong psychological pressures and physical torture on UN soldiers who were not trained to withstand such methods, and some of them gave in to their captors' demands. They occasionally found POWs who could be used to their advantage. Perhaps the germ warfare confessions were the result of the only true case of a man's mind being turned to his captor's will because the CCF succeeded in forcing UN pilots to sign confessions and make public propaganda statements about germ warfare operations that never happened. In counter-point, there were numerous cases in which men held out against interrogation or in which entire prison camps earned the respect of their jailers by standing together and resisting indoctrination.

To the educated Westerner, Communist indoctrination in the camps was crude and ineffective. Soldiers who had seen conditions in Korea were not impressed by the message that Communist society was the ideal. Men who had comfortable lives back home were not willing to abandon them for Communist poverty, social rigidity, and oppressive government.

Signed Leaflets

POWs also were used to sign leaflets. Often they were aimed at the American soldier. Here is one example:

> **American GIs. Have you ever stopped to think what you are fighting for? Stop! Just stop! And think it over! I say we shouldn't be fighting these people. I say we have no reason to fight these people whatsoever! We are fighting the people who are fighting for the freedom of their country. This is their country, not ours. We should withdraw from Korea. We're Americans. Let the Korean people settle their internal problems just as we settled ours.[3]**

The US POW whose signature was on the bottom of this document may have never known what he was signing. Some such signatures were forged from identification cards, ration books, and receipts for Red Cross parcels. There seemed to be enough genuine confessions and signed leaflet messages to go around, however, and US POWs were usually the ones the Communists exploited.

1. Perhaps the most complete volume on the Korean War POW is Eugene Kinkead's *Why They Collaborated* (New York: Longmans, 1959), a thought-provoking book. See also Max Hastings, *The Korean War* (New York: Simon and Schuster, 1987), pp. 297–98, and Callum A. MacDonald, *Korea: The War before Vietnam*, pp. 249–64.

2. This section was developed from several printed references and from personal interviews with US POWs. The POWs all agreed that a tough but nonconfrontational attitude was the most successful course. They also agreed that this took a lot of guts.

3. This is the text of an original leaflet bearing what was supposed to be a genuine appeal from a US POW.

8

Searchlights, Bugles, and All the Rest

Most wars seem to inspire inventive thinking, and the Korean War was no exception. Even a slight advantage over the enemy could translate into fewer casualties, and even victory. Both sides employed novel PSYWAR techniques.

SEARCHLIGHTS

Wild ideas sometimes work in wartime, no matter how imaginative they seem at first. Stopping the movement of Communist forces at night was a problem that plagued US commanders. Attacks on truck convoys at night using either flares or no illumination at all were somewhat successful, but a more controllable and long-term solution was sought. Eighty million-candlepower searchlights were used successfully during World War II aboard dirigibles for anti-submarine operations. The package was compact, considering the capacity of the lights, about the size of a napalm tank. Would it all fit under the wing of a B-26? During the summer of 1951, the 3rd and 452nd Wings of the Fifth Air Force mounted these Navy searchlights under B-26s. They increased drag (limiting the range of the bombers), started fires, and suffered other teething problems. Also, pilots thought the lights might direct ground fire their way. Still, the searchlights denied the enemy the cover of darkness, and the experiment continued.

During night intruder missions, the bombers would locate a convoy and mark the position with tracers and small fire-bombs or flares. Then they would switch on the searchlights— good for less than a minute of operation—and hit the convoy with 500-pound high-explosive bombs, 100-pound fragmentation bombs, and machine guns. The lights had serious psychological effects on the North Koreans. They felt exposed and would abandon their vehicles to the B-26 attack. Sometimes, after their ammo was exhausted, the bombers would make additional passes over the convoy with the searchlights on just to fray the nerves of the enemy. Although the searchlights were useful, keeping them in working order was a problem because they were too fragile to take the pounding while bolted to the bombers, and so they were withdrawn after four or five months of use. Captain John Walmsley was posthumously awarded the Medal of Honor for his actions during a B-26 searchlight mission.

Searchlights were more successful on the ground. Mounted on flatbed trucks with their own power supply, they were used to illuminate Communist positions. After several months' use, it was determined that shining the searchlights on low clouds rather than on the battlefield itself did a better job of illuminating a large area, and they were used in this manner on cloudy nights.

FIREFLY MISSIONS

Successful PSYWAR sometimes takes its cue from the interrogation of prisoners of war. After the Chinese intervention, prisoners told UN interrogators that they often depended on the cover of darkness for relocating forces. Major troop move-

Steven Rook

A large searchlight mounted on an Army flatbed truck.

ments were dangerous during the day because the United Nations had air supremacy and truck convoys were easy targets in daytime. Successful nighttime harassment would have serious psychological consequences on the Communist soldiers.[1]

Chinese military doctrine favored movements at night and they exploited this often. Wearing tennis shoes, the Chinese could move a large number of men and actually infiltrate UN lines before they were discovered. At the beginning of the war, UN aircraft never flew at night and observation posts were limited by the darkness. UN night intruder capabilities were limited because we had few night fighters. Aircraft needed to fly from forward bases so they could provide quick tactical support, but the airfields were too rough for the B-26s. They were used only for planned (non-emergency) missions since they had to be stationed at paved fields far from the front. The 3rd Wing (the former 21st TCS, now the 6461st) fitted their C-47s with flare chutes and assigned them to the 3rd Air Base Group at Taegu. Several aircraft were kept on alert at that base. Later, they were transferred to the 67th Tactical Reconnaissance Wing.

C-47s (and later some C-46s) were fitted with a chute to deploy naval Mark VIII flares, used by flying boat crews, in what was affectionately called a "wild idea." The flares ignited at 5,500 feet and burned for nearly five minutes, illuminating the ground to nearly daylight intensity. Trucks were then easily seen by the B-26s and could be attacked with bombs, rockets, napalm, and machine guns. UN troops also used the flares to illuminate maneuvers and readjustment of their positions. Prisoners captured after Firefly operations confirmed that flares severely inhibited their night movements, especially since they were often followed by medium-bomber attacks. Also, they were reluctant to attack UN positions when the Firefly planes were operating, afraid that flare aircraft would expose them. The flares usually worked well, but because the M-26 flares were too big for the C-47s, there was often a problem with duds.

During at least two-thirds of every month, the moon was such that enemy convoys had to use headlights. B-26s and Fire-fly C-47s would first observe the convoy to estimate its speed and direction and to see if it was near a crossroads. Then they would attack along its length, aiming first at the lead vehicles and those at the end to isolate and freeze the convoy on the road.

Such attacks against NKPA and CCF convoys were so successful that the Communists began trying to counter the low-flying aircraft. They established a special army group, the Hunters, whose job was to bring down the planes. Across valleys, Hunters strung steel cables that were impossible for the pilots to see. They faked convoys by stringing simulated headlights along a road to attract attacking planes, which would

Lee Jai Yong, a Korean "kicker," throws out a leaflet bundle from a C-47, September 1952. Note the flare chute (*right*) extending to the rear of the airplane for use during Firefly missions.

then be trapped by the cables and concentrated ground fire. The Firefly attacks kept coming and night travel was reduced, but the Communists were able to maintain their supply lines despite the Fireflies. The C-47s were considered too slow to survive far from the battle line, so the same naval flares were attached to the rocket rails on the wings of B-26s. The illumination was better than with the older M-26 flares, which were already part of the B-26's equipment, but there still were too many duds.

Though not officially part of Firefly operations, B-29s also dropped flares in support of medium-bomber missions, especially those after Inchon that were intended to destroy as much Communist equipment as possible. There were large convoys on the roads, especially at night. B-29s were instructed by General George Stratemeyer, the commanding general of the Far East Air Force (FEAF), to cooperate in night interdiction raids against them. A B-29 was detailed to carry a large load of M-26 parachute flares set to ignite above 5,000 feet. The B-29 circled over the general attack area and dispersed the flares, lighting a broad area. The B-26s then attacked the vehicles. During such an attack on 22 September 1950, the B-29s lighted a long highway and railway from Suwon to Kumchon. The B-26s destroyed numerous trucks and two trains, one of which continued to explode for more than half an hour.

On later missions, pairs of B-29s were teamed for night interdiction, one with flares, the other with fragmentation and small general-purpose bombs. The night attacks were limited by the short burning time of the World War II–vintage flares and their unreliability. One mission counted nearly 65 percent duds; one exploded prematurely, damaging the bomber. The missions with the M-26 flares were canceled. The British then supplied model 1950 flares, though in small numbers. The B-29 role was eventually canceled in favor of the Firefly missions, but the North Koreans learned to fear these attacks and they had a considerable psychological effect on them.

Another "wild idea" produced OPERATION TACK. The Firefly C-47s would drop flares to locate highways and then drop tons of nails to puncture the tires of the next convoy. After daylight, fighters could fly the same route as the Fireflies had the night before and strafe the crippled trucks. OPERATION TACK worked, but the CCF started using other methods to supply their troops (man- and horse-packing) and the "trap" didn't catch many targets. But the CCF had to rely on less effective methods to supply their troops or force their troops to find food locally. Night attacks weren't effective against mule convoys because the convoys didn't use roads or have lights. When Far East Air Material Command began manufacturing a four-pronged nail that would always have three barbs down like a tripod and one straight up, intended for wider use in Korea, the results were disappointing. With targets disappearing, the 3rd Wing was already cooling on the night attacks.

The Marines had better success than the Air Force or Army with coordinated Firefly missions, tallying three times the damage reported by the night intruders from the 3rd Wing. Flying Corsairs and Tiger Cats, they would rendezvous with a Firefly at dusk. The C-47 dropped its flares to the windward side of the target so their parachutes floated across the target area. The Marine aircraft carried 20mm cannons, napalm, 160-pound fragmentation bombs, 500-pound general-purpose bombs, and rockets. The cannons were the most useful. A C-47 could stay in the target area much longer than the fighters, so each Firefly served multiple waves of fighters. Finding the target in the dark was difficult. There were no major landmarks in the mountainous areas and navigational aids were rudimentary. Fighters and Fireflies would often fly low over the target area to draw fire to locate the enemy

The Communists relied on a spotter system to warn the convoys of a night intruder attack. The truck headlights could be seen going off as planes flew closer and on when the aircraft passed. Judging the results of an attack was difficult, since many targets were never visible. The pilots could only be sure they hit something when it blew up or caught fire. However, planners were sure, based on pilot and POW reports, that the Firefly-supported attacks were having a damaging psychological and supply effect on the Communists. They counted dozens of locomotives destroyed as well as many trucks, nearly 2,000 in one month alone. One of the best reports came from an airman who had been captured by the Chinese and was being transported to the North. He was in a convoy and managed to escape after a B-26 raid. He reported a general scene of chaos, destruction, and death.[2]

Firefly flights contributed strongly to OPERATION STRANGLE, a plan to totally interdict the enemy's lines of supply and isolate his frontline forces. The railways were the central target. Bridges and important intersections were also destroyed. Due to the success of the daytime STRANGLE mission, the roads and railways became clogged with traffic at night. Forcing the enemy to travel when the moon was low and to use his headlights made him easy pickings. The scene of a typical mission was said to look like a crowd leaving a football game.

Fireflies were also called on to support Army artillery. The Communists liked to attack at night, a standard Soviet army tactic. On 21 February 1953, I Corps tasked the Fireflies with flare coverage over the snow-covered Han River. Once, the flares revealed an attacking Communist army battalion, clearly outlined in the snow- and ice-covered river. While the aircraft kept the area illuminated, UN artillery pounded it with devastating results.

COMMUNIST BUGLES IN REVERSE

The Communists often used bugles as a communication device over small distances. They would signal troop movements with a short bugle tattoo and charge to a wild and rousing blast. They would sometimes use the bugles for PSYWAR effect by playing charge signals without charging. This was intended to fray the nerves of the defending UN troops and make them worry about a real charge. Sometimes, the Communists would blow bugles at night to disturb the defenders' sleep. After overrunning a UN position, they would blow taps for the dead and reveille for the living. UN troops tried to capture the bugles—which had a different sound than ours—and use them to foul up the enemy's signals. The Chinese also used whistles to signal their troops; UN forces tried to mimic them, too. These efforts had limited success but proved to be worthwhile irritants.

JAMES G. CHAPMAN, 223rd Inf Reg, 40th Div—On Christmas Eve, the Communist buglers tried to play "Jingle Bells" and "Silent Night" for the US troops.

USO SHOWS

USO shows and other well-intended events were certainly not PSYWAR tactics but sometimes had effects similar to those created by PSYWAR. The juxtaposition of a lively show and men dying on the battlefield could be more than some men could handle, resulting in depression or other psychological problems. Shows with pretty girls and music from back home often made the loneliness of soldiers more intense.

TOM DREW, D-2-7, 1st Marine Div—During our big battle on Bunker Hill, I got wounded early and went to a MASH unit just behind Jamestown. The Chinese were good and followed our jeep full of wounded with mortars right down the road. I was walking wounded. While waiting for my turn at the shrapnel table, I walked over into, of all things, a live USO show. Yes, the effect was rather dazzling. Moments from death, chased by mortars, and [here was] music, joy, and humor as personalities did their thing to allegedly brighten up the troops. I guess I must have been quite a sight as I walked up, still in full combat gear and spattered with good B-negative blood, to the front of the show. I didn't feel like getting cheered up. Post-trauma shock, I guess.

JAMES G. CHAPMAN, Co B, 223rd Inf Reg, 40th Div—One of the most depressing things that happened to our troops was to send them to the rear to be entertained by professionals after they had been psychologically battle hardened. I remember saying that if I were the enemy, I would pay American entertainers to play, on a weekly basis, the rifle companies. I believe this would be more detrimental to our frontline troops than any enemy propaganda, but the Army brass never realized this.

US INFORMATION SERVICE (USIS)

The USIS was the informational arm of the State Department.[3] Its mission was the Campaign of Truth, the worldwide effort to counter Communist propaganda with verifiable news and information about the United States and the democratic world. The two main media were Voice of America radio stations and the USIS press office. As soon as the North Koreans crossed the parallel, all USIS resources in Korea and Japan, including the VOA station in Manila, Philippines, were made available to the Far East Command and its Psychological Warfare Branch.

The Campaign of Truth had many facets. It sponsored exhibits about US life, culture, and industry. It booked tours for a wide range of US entertainers throughout the world to refute the Communist claim that the United States was a cultural desert. It sponsored visits by foreign businessmen to US factories.

The fast reaction of the United States and United Nations to support South Korea was dramatic proof to the world that they meant business. Early in the war, the USIS was the only agency with enough resources in the right place to perform consolidation PSYWAR. It was mobile, had small offices stocked with supplies throughout the country, and had translators ready. When the war started, Secretary of State Dean Acheson instituted a psychological strategy board led by Edward Barrnett. It began a study of North Korean and Chinese propaganda to identify trends that signaled policy changes. One trend was identified before the Chinese intervention. The Chinese began to talk about their role in defending North Korea weeks before they crossed the Yalu. Their home propaganda changed to reflect a stronger anti-US bias, calling on all Chinese to join the army to oust the Caucasian invaders.

After the Chinese crossed the Yalu, the VOA was the first US agency to announce it. On 2 November 1950, it reported: "The American X Corps announced that troops under its command were fighting a Chinese regiment. The announcement said the Chinese Communists were encountered thirty miles north of the port city of Hungnam. The X Corps described the regiment as wholly Chinese."

A later VOA news report said: "In an interview . . . General MacArthur said the Communists are apparently bringing into action 'a certain number of fresh troops' for the 'do-or-die attacks.' Earlier, General MacArthur's Headquarters disclosed that Communist reinforcements and supplies are coming from what was termed protected territory across the Yalu River."

After UN troops were successful in liberating areas, the State Department was responsible for initiating and carrying out consolidation PSYWAR there. It tried to assure civilians that they were better off under UN control and to demonstrate that truth. Credibility was a trademark of the information campaign. Any stupid statement or foolish stretching of the truth would do irreparable damage to the UN propaganda mission. It used radios, public address systems, bulletin board notices, newspaper tear sheets distributed by hand, leaflets, and movies to bring war and morale-building news to Koreans.

While the front lines trudged back and forth, USIS operations suffered badly, as did most of the Korean civilian infrastructures. USIS personnel always seemed to find themselves reoccupying burned-out facilities that they had evacuated only weeks before. They were always in need of equipment and local personnel, but they developed a reputation for rapid recovery after a forced move. This reputation led the Eighth Army to occasionally rely on them to produce translated radio and loudspeaker scripts and even leaflets for airdrops.

In the more stable areas of the country, USIS was able to publish a weekly poster and to improve its radio and loudspeaker news services. It cooperated with seven UN agencies in Korea, especially in the later years of the war.

1. Firefly/Lamplighter missions were often conducted in conjunction with loudspeaker and leaflet missions. See Robert Futrell, *The United States Air Force in Korea 1950–1953*, and the 315th unit history by Annis G. Thompson, *The Great Airlift*, for more coverage.

2. See Futrell, *The United States Air Force in Korea 1950–1953*.

3. The *Psychological Warfare Casebook* has many articles concerning the USIS. This organization is often overlooked in Korean War PSYWAR discussions, but it played an important part in consolidation PSYWAR.

AFTERWORD

PSYWAR was one of the first tactics used in the Korean War and one of the last. Between the North's initial attack and the armistice, UN forces fought their enemy on every imaginable battlefield, from night skies and beaches to frozen foxholes and the airwaves. They fought with obsolete aircraft, aging artillery, iron bombs, jellied gasoline, boomerang jets, and slips of paper. The fight was aimed against the mind as well as the body.

The enemy was fighting the war with the beginnings of Cold War tactics, the "future war." They used jets and mechanized forces that vastly increased the pace of the war. They expanded the front to include the international press, which broadened the conflict well beyond the fairly regional combat area. And the enemy used PSYWAR with an intense, scientifically designed program that was unlike anything seen before. We learned the lesson well and incorporated scientific PSYWAR into our Army doctrine.

The common soldier was told he was going to Korea for a "police action." What he found was an inhospitable foreign land and a real war against a brutal enemy that did not fight by our rules. Many veterans said they felt betrayed by the Army and abandoned by the American people. The soldier expected a safe bit of "policing" but instead found himself in a miserable war where people died, where the enemy executed its prisoners, and where captured Americans were used as psychological weapons.

The US soldier was unprepared to fight such a war. He was descended from the past war, but he was tasked to fight a future war, and the stakes were not what he expected. The war hurt all his senses, from smell and sight to the ability to feel heat and cold. It was fertile ground for the psychological soldier and his lies, leaflets, and loudspeakers.

DICK HUGHES, 21st TCS—I once talked to the mayor of Taegu after the Communists had been driven out of the city. He said he was busy trying to determine who was a Communist and who was not. Confirmed South Koreans were allowed to go home. Confirmed North Koreans were shot. "What do you do when you can't confirm if they are from the North or South?" I asked. He replied, "Oh, we shoot them, too."

GLOSSARY

AA: Antiaircraft
AFR: Air Force Regulation
AM: Air Medal
BCJ: Broadcasting Corporation of Japan
CCF: Communist Chinese Forces
CIA: Central Intelligence Agency
DFC: Distinguished Flying Cross
EUSAK: Eighth US Army, Korea
FEAF: Far East Air Force
FEC: Far East Command
GCA: Ground Control Approach
IP: Instruction pilot
KBS: Korean Broadcasting System
L&L: Loudspeaker and Leaflet
MLR: Main Line of Resistance
MSR: Main Supply Route
NKAF: North Korean Air Force
NKPA: North Korean People's Army
OCPW: Office of the Chief of Psychological Warfare
PI: Philippine Islands
POW: Prisoner of war
PSYWAR: Psychological warfare
PWB: Psychological Warfare Branch
PWD: Psychological Warfare Division
PWS: Psychological Warfare Section
RB&L: Radio Broadcasting and Leaflet
RCT: Regimental Combat Team
ROK: Republic of Korea

SAM: Special Air Missions
STOL: Short takeoff and landing
VOA: Voice of America
VUNC: Voice of the United Nations Command
WAC: Women's Army Corps

SOURCES

The Korean War has not been well documented, and psychological warfare even less so. Like the title of Clay Blair's book, Korea was *The Forgotten War.* The books listed below all contributed to this work. Major references are marked with an asterisk. I am also deeply indebted to personal letters from former Korean War pilots, soldiers, and sailors.

Appleman, Roy E. *South to the Naktong, North to the Yalu.* Washington, DC: Government Printing Office, 1986.

Atkinson, James David. *The Edge of War.* Chicago: H. Regnery, 1960.

*Barnett, Frank R., and Carnes Lord, eds. *Political Warfare and Psychological Operations: Rethinking the US Approach.* Washington, DC: National Defense University Press, 1989.

Barnett, Frank R., B. Hugh Tovar, and Richard H. Shultz, eds. *Special Operations in US Strategy.* Washington, DC: Government Printing Office, National Defense University Press, 1984.

Barrnett, Edward W. *Truth Is Our Weapon.* New York: Funk and Wagnalls, 1953.

*Berger, Carl. *An Introduction to Wartime Leaflets.* Washington, DC: Special Operations Research Office, American University, 1959.

———. *B-29: The Superfortress.* New York: Ballentine, 1970.

Blair, Clay. *The Forgotten War: America in Korea 1950-1953.* New York: Times Books, 1987.

Brown, Wallace. *The Endless Hours: My Two and a Half Years as a Prisoner of the Chinese Communists.* New York: Norton, 1961.

*Cagle, Commander Malcolm W., and Commander Frank A. Manson. *The Sea War in Korea.* Annapolis, MD: US Naval Institute, 1957.

*Clark, General Mark. *From the Danube to the Yalu.* New York: Harper & Bros., 1954, 1988.

*Clauser, Jerome K. *Voice of the United Nations Command (VUNC): A Description of a Strategic Radio Broadcasting Psychological Operation.* US Army Research Organization, August 1971.

*Daughtery, William, ed. *Psychological Warfare Casebook.* Baltimore: Operations Research Office, Johns Hopkins, 1958.

Final Report on F-86D versus MIG-15. Eglin Air Force Base, FL: Air Proving Ground Command, 22 November 1954.

Flexible Air Transport. HQ 315th Air Division (Combat Cargo), APO 959, 15 November 1951.

*Futrell, Robert Frank. *The United States Air Force in Korea 1950–1953.* New York: Duell, Sloan and Pearce, 1961.

Gallant, Roy. "More Psycho than Logical." *The Reporter.* 31 March 1953, pp. 17–19.

———. "Why Red Troops Surrender in Korea." *The Reporter.* 5 August 1952, pp. 19–21.

Giangreco, D. M. *War in Korea 1950–1953.* Novato, CA: Presidio, 1990.

Goulden, Joseph C. *Korea: The Untold Story of the War.* New York: Times Books, 1982.

*Harris, Elliot. *The "Un-American" Weapon.* New York: M. W. Lads, 1967.

*Hastings, Max. *The Korean War.* New York: Simon and Schuster, 1987.

Kinkead, Eugene. *Why They Collaborated.* New York: Longmans, 1959.

Langer, William L. *An Encyclopedia of World History.* Boston: Houghton Mifflin, 1980.

*Linebarger, Paul M. A. *Psychological Warfare.* Washington,

DC: Infantry Journal Press, 1948, 1954.

MacDonald, Callum A. *Korea: The War before Vietnam*. New York: The Free Press/Macmillan, 1986.

Owen, David. *Battle of Wits: History of Psychology and Deception in Modern Warfare*. London: Leo Cooper, 1978.

*Paddock, Alfred H., Jr. *US Army Special Warfare: Its Origins; Psychological and Unconventional Warfare, 1941–1952*. Washington, DC: National Defense University Press, 1982.

*Pollock, Daniel C., ed., and others. *The Art and Science of Psychological Operations: Case Studies of Military Application*. US Army Pamphlet 525-7-1 and -2. Washington, DC: Government Printing Office, 1976.

"Psychological Warfare in Korea, An Interim Report," *Public Opinion Quarterly*, spring 1951, pp. 65–75.

Ranelagh, John. *The Agency: The Rise and Decline of the CIA*. New York: Touchstone, 1987.

Roetter, Charles. *The Art of Psychological Warfare, 1914–1945*. New York: Stein and Day, 1954, 1974.

Ruffner, Frederick C., Jr., and Robert C. Thomas. *Code Name Dictionary*. Detriot, MI: Grale Research, 1963.

Summers, Colonel Harry G. *Korean War Almanac*. New York: Facts on File, 1990.

*Thompson, Captain Annis G. *The Greatest Airlift: The Story of Combat Cargo*. Tokyo: 315th Air Division, May 1954.

*Watson, Peter. *War on the Mind*. New York: Basic Books, 1978.

Weigley, Russell F. *The American Way of War*. Bloomington, IN: Indiana University Press, 1973.

Williams, Peter, and David Wallace. *Unit 731: Japan's Secret Biological Warfare in World War II*. New York: The Free Press, 1989.

Yeager, General Chuck and Leo Janos. *Yeager, An Autobiography*. New York: Bantam Books, 1985.

Zook, David H., and Robin Higham. *A Short History of Warfare*. New York: Twayne, 1966.

APPENDIX A

F-86D vs. MIG-15
The Official Report

OPERATION MOOLAH offered $100,000 for any Communist pilot who flew a Soviet-made jet fighter to South Korea. The intent was to capture the latest in Soviet technology, but there also was a PSYWAR objective. If the Communists feared their pilots might accept the offer, they might limit their fighter operations. Although the evidence isn't perfectly clear, there was a downturn in Communist MIG sorties after General Mark Clark broadcast the offer. After Captain Ro Kum Suk flew his MIG-15bis to Kimpo, the aircraft was secretly taken to Okinawa for testing versus the F-86. One of the test pilots was Chuck Yeager, who has an excellent, firsthand account of the testing in his autobiography.

This report was originally classified secret on 10 December 1954, but was unclassified on 15 December 1960. It is reproduced here with the original marking as far as possible. A copy of the original is in the Air Force Academy library's open collection.

HEADQUARTERS
AIR PROVING GROUND COMMAND
Eglin Air Force Base, Florida

This material contains information affecting the national defense
of the United States within the meaning of the Espionage Laws,
Title 18, U.S.C. Sections 793 and 794, the transmission or revela-
tion of which in any manner to an unauthorized person is prohibited
by law.

FINAL REPORT
ON
F-86D VERSUS MIG-15
PROJECT NO. APG/ADA/49-A-1

This document is classified secret in
accordance with paragraph 23C, AFR 205-1

Additional copies of this Report may be obtained from
Armed Services Technical Information Agency
Document Service Center
Knott Building, Dayton 2, Ohio

Indicate Project Number and Title

Distribution Limitations:

This document will not be distributed outside the Department of
Defense or its contractors without prior approval of this Headquarters.

Retain or destroy in accordance with AFR 205-1. Do not return.

Copy No. 58 of 300 copies

HEADQUARTERS
AIR PROVING GROUND COMMAND
Eglin Air Force Base, Florida
22 November 1954

PROJECT NO. APG/ADA/49-A-1
F-86D Versus MIG-15

1. This is the Final Report on Project No. APG/ADA/49-A-1, the object of which was to determine the capability of the F-86D in a fighter versus fighter role against a MIG-15 type aircraft. The limited amount of flying time on the MIG-15 available for this test precluded a comprehensive investigation of the capabilities of each aircraft against the other. Rather, a limited test was conducted to determine tactics which will minimize the effectiveness of MIG-15 attacks against F-86D aircraft. (C)

2. Additional tests were conducted involving MIG-15 attacks against B-36, B-47, and F-84F aircraft; results of these tests are reported separately in Projects No. APG/SAA/167-A-1, 2, and 3 respectively. Tracking capabilities of the AN/FPS-3 search radar against the MIG-15 are reported under Project No. APG/SAA/167-A-4. (U)

3. It is recommended that the tactics outlined in this report be considered in theaters where F-86D Interceptors will be required to operate within the range of MIG-15 type aircraft. (C)

PATRICK W. TIMBERLAKE
Major General, USAF
Commander

HEADQUARTERS
AIR FORCE BASE OPERATIONAL TEST CENTER
Eglin Air Force Base, Florida

SUBJECT: Final Report on Project No. APG/ADA/49-A-1,
F-86D versus MIG-15 (U)

1. Introduction:

Employment of the F-86D fighter-interceptor is planned in theatres of operation where encounters with high performance enemy day fighters may be expected during normal bomber interception mission. Project APG/ADA/49-A-1 was initiated at the direction of the Commander, APGC under the provisions of AFR 80-14. This project consists of a brief evaluation of the operational impact of the MIG-15 upon the mission of the F-86D during day VFR conditions. Consideration of the capabilities of the F-86D as an air superiority fighter was not included. (C)

2. Test Conditions:

a. The F-86D-5 aircraft was flown without external loads. Full internal fuel and rockets were carried on each sortie. The MIG-15 was equipped with the VK-1 engine and flown at normal take-off weight, in a clean configuration. (C)

b. Three missions were flown during the conduct of the test. Formation take-offs and climbs were made to altitude and comparative maneuvers were executed. (U)

3. Test Results:

a. Acceleration runs were made at 35,000 feet, with both aircraft stabilized at .82 Mach at the beginning of each run. During this maneuver, the F-86D gradually pulled away from the MIG-15, but the difference in acceleration is so slight that it is considered of little tactical significance, but there was a level flight speed advantage of approximately 15 knots. (S)

b. Comparative climbs were made from sea level to 40,000' at the optimum climb speed of the F-86D. Under these conditions the F-86D could easily climb away from the MIG-15. Above this altitude, this advantage rapidly diminished and could not be relied upon as a defensive maneuver. (S)

c. Straight and level runs were made by the F-86D at .85 to .9 Mach with the MIG-15 situated above and to the side on an attack run. During the firing pass, the F-86D executed a violent break in the direction of the attack and made a diving turn using A/B. The MIG-15 was unable to track during this maneuver, even when the F-86D reversed the turn away to simulate a heading for return to base or reattack. This was attributed to the poor control characteristics of the MIG-15 above .90 Mach. When evading action was not taken by the F-86D, the MIG-15 was able to complete attacks successfully. (S)

d. The F-86D was unable to avoid successful attacks by the MIG-15 by attempting level turning maneuvers at speeds of .8 to .9 Mach. No attempt was made to simulate attack runs by the F-86D against the MIG-15. (S)

4. Collective Analysis:

When considering the capability of the F-86D operating in day VFR conditions against a bomber force defended by MIG-15 type fighters, it is apparent that beam or slight forward of the beam lead-collision course attacks at high speed offer the lowest probability of compromise by escorting fighters. Positioning of the escorting MIG-15's for defense against this type of attack would have to be well forward and to either side of the bombers before the F-86D could be detected in time to interrupt his attack. Conversely, any lead-collision course attack conducted behind the beam around to the tail of the bomber would become progressively more hazardous. However, when the F-86D pilot is faced with the problem of multiple bombers, escort and friendly fighters, in the same area, target discrimination may become impossible, thus precluding firing in the automatic function. In this event, it might be necessary to revert to day fighter tactics in the stern quarter and use visual firing methods. (S)

5. Conclusions:

a. If the MIG-15 has altitude and position advantage, it can force the F-86D to abort a lead-collision intercept, even with the F-86D at maximum effective attack speed (approximately .9 M). (S)

b. The F-86D can evade the MIG-15, even though the latter is in firing position. The best evasive maneuver is a tight diving turn using maximum power until out of firing range. (S)

6. Recommendations:

The results of this test be considered in the planning of F-86D combat operations. (U)

7. This document is classified Secret in accordance with paragraph 23c, AFR 205-1. (U)

W. B. PUTNAM
Colonel, USAF
Commander

APPENDIX B

1st Loudspeaker and Leaflet Company Report

The 1st Loudspeaker and Leaflet Company was the tactical PSYWAR unit for the Eighth Army and the United Nations in Korea. This monthly report for May 1952 was originally classified secret by the Far East Command, but was unclassified by Executive Order 12356, Section 3.3, and released 9 January 1991. It is copied here with errors in spelling and grammar included. The report is interesting in that it shows the scope of the 1st L&L's mission. During May 1951, it printed almost eight million leaflets despite serious supply and equipment problems. Remember, the war was less than a year old at the time this report was written. It is interesting that PSYWAR was credited with nearly 3,000 prisoners during the month.

GENERAL HEADQUARTERS
FAR EAST COMMAND

APO 500

AG 314.7 (14 Jun 51) GB   **16 Jun 51**
SUBJECT: Transmittal of Command Report (RCS CSHIS-5(RI))

TO: The Adjutant General
Department of the Army
Washington 25, D. C.
ATTENTION: AGAO-S

Forwarded herewith in compliance with AR 345-105, 3 October 1950, are two (2) copies of Command Report for 1st Loudspeaker and Leaflet Company, Army, APO 301, Taegu, Korea, for the period May 1951.

FOR THE COMMANDER-IN-CHIEF:

1 Incl
Cmd Rpt (2) copies   C. A. BARNES
                                                Lt Col, AGC
                                                Asst Adj Gen

1st Loudspeaker and Leaflet
Company, Army, APO 301
Taegu, Korea

Command Report No. 5
Period Covered: May 51

COMMAND REPORT

1. Introduction

a. During the period the 1st Loudspeaker and Leaflet Company continued under direct control of the Psychological Warfare Section (G-3 Section) EUSAK. There were no major changes of an administrative or operational nature. Continuous efforts were made to remedy the supply problems e.g. the shortage of essential items of equipment. By the close of the period considerable improvement was in evidence.

2. Personnel

a. The company entered the period with a strength figure of eight (8) officers and ninety-three (93) enlisted men. By the close of the period this figure was seven (7) officers and one hundred three (103) enlisted men. Captain William F. Kingry (Publications Platoon) sustained injuries to his knee and was evacuated to Japan for further treatment. Officer is tentatively expected to return to duty 15 June 1951.

b. The problem of equipping indigenous Chinese linguists working with the Loudspeaker Platoon had still not been solved at the close of the period.

3. Training

a. Training was accomplished in connection with operations, and is a continual process for new and inexperienced personnel assigned as replacements. Efficiency in all platoons, more specifically the Publications Platoon, has increased considerably as more and better equipment became available.

4. Organization

(no change)

5. Orders and Missions
(no change)

6. Operations
  a. Publication Platoon
    (1) Processing Section
      (a) No artillery ammunition was loaded with leaflets during the period.
      (b) The principal operation of the Processing Section during the period was the cutting of paper stock, and the packaging and delivery of leaflets. The necessity of using a Korean paper cutter was still impairing the efficiency of this section at close of the period.
    (2) Press Section
      (a) The following leaflets were printed by the Press Section, 1 May to 31 May:

Leaflet #8032 ──────────────	200,000	Black 5X7
Leaflet #8103 ──────────────	250,000	Black 5X7
Leaflet #8122 ──────────────	180,000	Black 5X7
Break-down on Leaflet #8122		
47th CCF ──────────────	90,000	
48th CCF ──────────────	90,000	
Leaflet #8123 ──────────────	300,000	Black 5X7
Leaflet #8125 ──────────────	500,000	Black 5X7
Leaflet #8128 ──────────────	300,000	Black 5X7
Leaflet #8520 ──────────────	600,000	Black 5X7
Leaflet #8524 ──────────────	500,000	Black 5X7
Leaflet #8527 ──────────────	500,000	Black 5X7
Leaflet #8529 ──────────────	1,000,000	Red 3-7/16X7-7/16
Leaflet #8529 Rerun ─────────	900,000	Red 3-7/16X7-7/16
Leaflet #8544 ──────────────	300,000	Black 5X7
Leaflet #8532 ──────────────	500,000	Black 5X7
Leaflet #8533 ──────────────	500,000	Black 5X7
Leaflet #8535 ──────────────	500,000	Black 5X7

Leaflet #8536 ————————	600,000	Black 5X7
Break-down on Leaflet #8536		
15th CCF —————————	200,000	
20th CCF —————————	200,000	
12th CCF —————————	200,000	

Leaflet Total ————————— **7,930,000**

(b) The above figure exceeds total of previous month by 5,260,000 leaflets.

(c) The main difficulties arising in the Press Section during the period are listed as follows:

1. A shortage of paper stock caused a three day delay, however, the time lost in printing was utilized to good advantage in the installation of the Harris LTV and Davidson presses in a new and larger building recently constructed for this purpose.

2. Davidson press #3 was inoperative temporarily due to damage in shipment. Necessary repairs were effected by the 38th Ordnance Medium Maintenance Company. The assistance of this unit has been extremely helpful in the maintenance of presses and other allied equipment.

3. Harris press #1 remains inoperative as of 18 April due to lack of replacement parts. Some replacement parts have been received, the additional parts required to place this press in operation are presently not available, but are on "Back-Order" through Engineer channels.

4. Red inks continued to cause delay, and it was necessary to discontinue use of present stocks due to hardening because of age. Fresh stocks are on requisition.

5. Paper stocks are in good supply, and re-supply arrangements, on the basis of 2400 reams (22 x 34 inches) per ninety (90) day period have been made through Quartermaster channels.

(3) Camera and Plate Section

(a) Although this unit is now in receipt of a plate grainer, lack of required expendable supplies necessitated continued use of plate graining facilities supplied by the 8038th Engineer Topo

Company and the 62nd Engineer Topo Company. Although use of these facilities has been very helpful, the limited number of plates regrained in this manner was a matter of much concern at the close of the period.

(b) The principal difficulties encountered were as follows:

1. A two (2) day delay due to lack of egg albumen required in sensitizing plates prior to burning.

2. Extreme hot weather has necessitated the processing of film negatives only during the hours 2200 to 1000, causing considerable delay on priority work.

(c) The receipt of a new Galley type copying camera, a vacuum printing frame, and a carbon type twin arc lamp for burning plates, has increased the efficiency of the section considerably.

b. Propaganda Platoon

(1) The operations of the propaganda platoon consisted of writing leaflets, assisting in dissemination of leaflets, and necessary operations required to assure coordination of projects from the time the leaflets is approved until it is either air-dropped or distributed by artillery shells. The propaganda platoon also made recordings of Prisoners of War programs for "Voice of America" broadcasts during this period.

(2) Eighteen leaflets were dropped during the month, designed and written by the Projects Section, Psywar, EUSAK, of which the Propaganda Platoon of the 1st Loudspeaker and Leaflet Company is an integral part.

(3) The following leaflets in which this section assisted in the preparation and dissemination of, are listed below:

NUMBER	TYPE	DATE DROPPED
8523	Chinese Anti-Morale	3 May 51
8524	Chinese Anti-Morale	4 May 51
8527	Chinese Anti-Morale	7 May 51
8513	Chinese Official Safe Conduct Pass	9 May 51
8529	Chinese Currency Safe Conduct Pass	10 May 51
8525	Chinese Good Treatment	10 May 51
8125	NK Anti-Morale	11 May 51

NUMBER	TYPE	DATE DROPPED
8123	NK Anti-Morale	13 May 51
8522	Chinese Anti-Morale	13 May 51
8526	Chinese Anti-Morale	18 May 51
8524	Chinese Anti-Morale	19 May 51
8535	Chinese Anti-Morale	19 May 51
8537	Chinese Anti-Morale	19 May 51
8520	Chinese Anti-Morale	20 May 51
8532	Chinese Anti-Morale	24 May 51
8533	Chinese Anti-Morale	24 May 51
8534	Chinese Surrender Appeal	24 May 51
8536	Chinese Anti-Morale	24 May 51
8547	Chinese Anti-Morale	28 May 51

c. Loudspeaker Platoon

(1) At the close of the period, the strength of the platoon was four (4) officers and twenty-six (26) enlisted personnel.

(2) The platoon CP at Yoju air-strip continued to service and repair the vehicles and loudspeaker equipment. Nine (9) teams operated during the period with all American divisions, and with other United Nations forces, conducting a total of forty-eight (48) missions.

(3) Experiments were conducted with the AN/UIQ-1, public address set, including the use of a British Bren Carrier as an amplifier mount, and remote operation of the speaker unit up to one half (½) mile from the amplifiers. The AN/TIQ-7 public address set was thoroughly tested, both on the ground and in a light (L-19) aircraft. The AN/TIQ-7 public address set is considered limited in application as compared with the AN/UIQ-1 public address set, for the following reasons:

(a) Lacks required durability for extensive field use.

(b) Precise lubrication of air compression unit difficult to maintain under field conditions.

1. Carbon vanes used in air compression unit not presently available through normal supply channels.

(c) The safety factor for operating personnel under combat conditions is decreased due to inherent physical characteristics e.g. the operator must be in close proximity to the set in order to maintain control.

(4) A known total of two thousand nine hundred forty three (2943) prisoners surrendered as a direct result of ground loudspeaker broadcasts. This is a considerable increase over the preceding period. Prisoner of War interrogation reports received at the close of the period indicate that seventy-four (74) percent of all POW screened were influenced by Psywar activities, and mass surrenders are increasingly numerous.

(5) Three AN/UIQ-1 amplifiers were deadlined during the period due to lack of certain replacement parts. As soon as necessary repairs are effected, the 10th loudspeaker team will be placed in operation, bringing the platoon to 83% of its authorized number of loudspeaker teams.

(6) Tape recorder-reproducers (RD-74/U) were made available for the use of the loudspeaker platoon near the close of the period. One loudspeaker team has been equipped with a recorder-reproducer and tape recordings in lieu of a linguist, however, field reports on the effectiveness of this equipment were not available at the close of the period.

7. Intelligence
(no change)

8. Planning
a. Receipt of additional items of T/O&E equipment and continued improvement in training and operational techniques, has enabled the unit to gauge its capabilities more precisely, and facilitate planning. The lack of essential items of equipment and certain expendable supplies, still necessitate substitution and experimentation to some extent, however, this situation is rapidly being overcome, as equipment and supplies become more readily available.

9. Administration
(no change)

10. Logistics
a. Logistics continued to be the largest single problem in the unit. The continual effort being made to alleviate this condition had shown positive results by the end of the period, however, consider-

able improvement is still necessary in order to effect full and efficient operation.

b. A plate grainer was made available to the unit through Engineer channels, however, lack of the required expendable supplies prevented use of this equipment at the close of the period.

c. Authority was granted by the EUSAK Engineer to issue two (2) 30 KW diesel driven power generators to this unit. These units were not available at the close of the period.

d. A power driven paper cutter is tentatively expected to be made available to the unit through Quartermaster channels by 10 June.

e. A small detachment (2 EM) remained in Pusan during the period to expedite delivery of equipment and supplies arriving from Japan, and additional equipment and supplies on requisition with the various Pusan Supply Depots.

11. Morale

a. Morale continued very good to excellent during the period.

DONALD W. OSGOOD
Major   Inf
Commanding

INDEX